CONVERTED

CON VER TED

TRUE Mormon Conversion **STORIES** from **15** RELIGIONS

ALONZO L. GASKILL

CFI
An Imprint of Cedar Fort, Inc.
Springville, Utah

This is not an official publication of The Church of Jesus Christ of Latter-day Saints. The opinions and views expressed herein belong solely to the author and do not necessarily represent the opinions or views of Cedar Fort, Inc. Permission for the use of sources, graphics, and photos is also solely the responsibility of the author.

ISBN 13: 978-1-4621-2008-6

Published by CFI, an imprint of Cedar Fort, Inc.,
2373 W. 700 S., Springville, UT 84663
Distributed by Cedar Fort, Inc., www.cedarfort.com

LIBRARY OF CONGRESS CATALOGING-IN-PUBLICATION DATA

Names: Gaskill, Alonzo L., author.
Title: Converted : true mormon conversion stories from 15 religions / Alonzo L. Gaskill.
Description: Springville, UT : CFI, an imprint of Cedar Fort, Inc., [2017] | Includes bibliographical references and index.
Identifiers: LCCN 2016055838 | ISBN 9781462120086 (hardback : alk. paper)
Subjects: LCSH: Mormon converts--Biography.
Classification: LCC BX8693 .G37 2017 | DDC 248.2/419332--dc23
LC record available at https://lccn.loc.gov/2016055838

Cover design by Shawnda T. Craig
Cover design © 2017 by Cedar Fort, Inc.
Edited and typeset by Rebecca Bird

Printed in the United States of America

10 9 8 7 6 5 4 3 2 1

Printed on acid-free paper

In appreciation of all those
who openly and faithfully live their religion;
And in honor of all who embrace the truth,
regardless of the personal costs.

OTHER BOOKS BY ALONZO L. GASKILL

KNOW YOUR RELIGIONS VOLUME 1:
A COMPARATIVE LOOK AT MORMONISM AND CATHOLICISM

SACRED SYMBOLS:
FINDING MEANING IN RITES, RITUALS, AND ORDINANCES

THE LOST LANGUAGE OF SYMBOLISM: AN ESSENTIAL GUIDE FOR
RECOGNIZING AND INTERPRETING SYMBOLS OF THE GOSPEL

THE TRUTH ABOUT EDEN:
UNDERSTANDING THE FALL AND OUR TEMPLE EXPERIENCE

LOVE AT HOME:
INSIGHTS FROM THE LIVES OF LATTER-DAY PROPHETS

THE LOST TEACHINGS OF JESUS
ON THE SACRED PLACE OF WOMEN

MIRACLES OF THE NEW TESTAMENT:
A GUIDE TO THE SYMBOLIC MESSAGES

ODDS ARE, YOU'RE GOING TO BE EXALTED:
EVIDENCE THAT THE PLAN OF SALVATION WORKS!

REMEMBER:
SACRED TRUTHS WE MUST NEVER FORGET

MIRACLES OF THE BOOK OF MORMON:
A GUIDE TO THE SYMBOLIC MESSAGES

TEMPLE REFLECTIONS:
INSIGHTS INTO THE HOUSE OF THE LORD

CONTENTS

INTRODUCTION 1

AMISH: ABE HOCHSTETLER 5

ATHEIST: DANIEL ORTNER 19

BAPTIST: BRYAN READY 29

BUDDHIST: KANOKPHOL "YOUNG" LIMPANASRIPHONG 43

EPISCOPALIAN AND LUTHERAN: MEREDITH AND RANDALL CASTO . . .53

EVERYTHING: KEONGUK KIM 65

HINDU: ARUNA PICHHIIKA 75

JEHOVAH'S WITNESS: LEE NOBLEMAN 87

JUDAISM: MITCH COWITZ 97

MUSLIM: NAZEERA BEGUM PATHAN 107

CONTENTS

GREEK ORTHODOX: ALONZO L. GASKILL 119

RE-CONVERSION: KEVIN WILSON 131

REORGANIZED CHURCH OF JESUS CHRIST OF LATTER DAY SAINTS:
DENNIS CATO 141

ROMAN CATHOLIC: BEVERLY MARBEN 153

ABOUT THE COMPILER 167

INTRODUCTION

I n July 2016, Cedar Fort approached me about compiling a book of conversion stories of people who are former practitioners of other religions but have found the restored gospel of Jesus Christ. For a number of reasons—including the fact that I, myself, am a convert to the Church—the project sounded intriguing to me, so I agreed to be the editor of the volume.

In many ways, this compilation is eclectic, as each of the conversion stories shared herein is unique. Some of the authors were formerly members of other Christian churches but gained a testimony of the further light and knowledge found in The Church of Jesus Christ of Latter-day Saints. Others who shared their stories and witnesses in this volume have converted from non-Christian traditions, such as Hinduism, Buddhism, Islam, and Judaism. Each person joined the Church for various reasons—and each was converted through very different means; nevertheless, each story testifies to the joy that has come through embracing the restored gospel. All have found that their lives have been significantly changed and bettered because of Christ and the Restoration of His gospel in the latter days.

In His parable of the treasure hidden in a field (Matthew 13:44), Jesus taught, "The kingdom of heaven is like unto treasure hid in a field;

the which when a man hath found, he . . . selleth all that he hath, and buyeth that field." As the parable suggests, the gospel is priceless. Those truly converted to it are willing to give *anything required* in order to have it. While many of the stories in this volume attest to the tremendous blessings that have come through joining the Church, they also testify to the reality that conversion can require great sacrifice too. I am in awe of the tens of thousands of converts who, over the decades, have forfeited family and fortune in order to embrace Jesus and His restored gospel. The clarion call of the convert is often one of sacrifice. In their book *The Mormon Experience*, Leonard J. Arrington and Davis Bitton note:

> Mormon family life [particularly in the early years of the Restoration] often included experiences not easily disregarded—actual life as opposed to beliefs. For one thing, there was the original conversion to Mormonism, which often meant the schism of families. In the sense that it was virtually impossible to bring all of one's extended family into the new faith, some kind of religious separation was inevitable. The tears and heartache that followed such division, especially when it occurred in the immediate family, are incalculable.[1]

Many of the stories in this book exemplify this kind of sacrifice. Unquestionably, God sends compensating blessings to those who give all in order to be faithful disciples of Jesus Christ; and, for that, we offer our sincere praise! But conversion often requires great change and, thus, also requires tremendous faith. Your own experience may evidence that. Certainly many of the experiences shared in this volume do.

Of course, becoming a member of the Church—whether through a convert baptism, or by baptism when eight years old—is merely the gate (see 2 Nephi 31:17). There is a long path that leads from that initial salvific ordinance to the celestial kingdom. Converts need to remember this and give themselves time to grow and become perfected in Christ (see Moroni 10:32). Similarly, those who have been lifelong members need to

> UNQUESTIONABLY, GOD SENDS **COMPENSATING BLESSINGS** TO THOSE WHO GIVE ALL IN ORDER TO BE **FAITHFUL DISCIPLES** OF JESUS CHRIST.

remember that our convert brothers and sisters need time to grow into their newfound faith. Elder Bruce R. McConkie counseled, "Staunch and stable members of the Church should be tolerant and charitable toward persons newly coming out of the darkness of the world into the light of the gospel."[2]

In other words, when someone is investigating the Church, or has recently converted, those who have been in the Church many years need to be patient with the new convert or investigator as he or she learns the doctrines, incorporates the new lifestyle, and let's go of any erroneous perspectives from the past. When we do not exhibit such patience, we run the risk of pushing away recent converts. As a singular example, I knew of a woman who—with her husband—had converted to The Church of Jesus Christ of Latter-day Saints from Methodism. The sister dressed modestly, but, in that first year of membership in the Church, often wore skirts that were above her knee. One day a well-meaning sister pulled her aside and said, "Your skirts are too short." Choosing to not take offense, the recent convert quipped, "Oh, you'll have to excuse me. My husband and I are now LDS, but my skirts are all still Methodist!"

> MY HUSBAND AND I ARE NOW **LDS**, BUT MY SKIRTS ARE ALL STILL **METHODIST!**

Fortunately, this exchange did not push the recent convert away from the Church—*but it could have*. We should love, nurture, and accept those who are investigating the Church and those who have recently converted to it. Indeed, we should love, nurture, and accept *all* members because we don't know where they're at in their relationship with the Lord. We should have patience with less-active members, supporting them as they try to find their faith. We should give all members time to become what the Lord wants them to be—just as we would want the Lord to give *us* time to become what He wants *us* to be.

Finally, Elder Richard G. Scott reminded members of the Church that "your happiness now and forever is conditioned on your degree of conversion and the transformation that it brings to your life."[3] The degree to which we fully embrace Christ's teachings and commands is the degree to which we will find the gospel a blessing and strength in our lives. The various converts who have freely shared their stories herein have each learned—to one degree or another—that the more one consecrates one's life to Christ and His kingdom, the more blessed one will be. May the various stories of faith and sacrifice shared herein give each of us a renewed commitment to fully live our covenants and openly live our faith, that the blessings of God may be ours—and that we might be a blessing in the lives of others.

ALONZO L. GASKILL

NOTES

1. Leonard J. Arrington and Davis Bitton, *The Mormon Experience* (Illinois: University of Illinois Press, 1992), 193.
2. Bruce R. McConkie, *Doctrinal New Testament Commentary* (Salt Lake City: Bookcraft, 1971), 2:184.
3. Richard G. Scott, "Full Conversion Brings Happiness," *Ensign*, May 2002.

AMISH

ABE HOCHSTETLER

Being born Amish wasn't really hard for me. It just happened sort of naturally. I was one of thirteen children: nine boys and four girls. I always felt that growing up in such a large family was good for me, since it taught me how to deal with both older and younger siblings.

My parents taught me at an early age that it was okay to enjoy life—to have fun with whatever came your way. To really understand me, you need to know that I'm a bit of a joker. I enjoy a good laugh—though that's come back to haunt me a few times. I specifically remember one incident where my mother played a practical joke on me, the lasting effects of which are with me to this day. It happened to be my birthday, and I had been outside. From the kitchen, my mother called to me to come inside. After entering the house, she informed me that my older brother had sent over a present for me. I noticed that there was a small white box sitting on the table. It seemed odd at the time, because I very rarely received any-thing for my birthday. Had I known what was in store for me, I probably would not have opened it. I didn't realize it, but that day my father had slaughtered some pigs, and my mother had taken one of the pig eyes and put it in the box. To this day, I am a bit leery of birthday presents.

I had a great relationship with my grandfather, for whom I am named. Between my father and my grandfather (whom we called "Opa"),

I learned at an early age to love reading the Bible. Nearly every evening, I would spend an hour or two reading God's word. These evenings of reading the scriptures laid an excellent foundation for me: a foundation that would bear fruit in the future. Reading the scriptures enforced in my mind and heart the practical value of the Bible as a guidebook for one's life. (Too many today neglect application of that book's teachings and, consequently, make a lot of missteps in life.)

READING THE **SCRIPTURES** ENFORCED IN MY MIND AND HEART THE PRACTICAL VALUE OF THE **BIBLE AS A GUIDEBOOK** FOR ONE'S LIFE.

Reading the Bible as much as I did, I started to notice that there were some things that felt to me like doctrinal discrepancies—particularly in the New Testament. I talked pretty openly with my father and grandfather about the scriptures and what I was reading and learning. When I questioned the things that didn't make sense to me, my father and grandfather would always retort, "You can have any opinion you want in private, but in public, your opinion needs to match the bishop's." This didn't always set right with me. In ways, it provoked some doubts—and certainly some frustration. Naturally, I couldn't really do anything about it because I was Amish. Thus, I firmly believed that I was one of God's children and that being born Amish gave me a spiritual advantage over the non-Amish (or the "English," as the Amish call them). Truth be told, I felt luckier (or more blessed) than most, as they had to live the life of the English.

One Amish teaching that I really took issue with was the belief that God was triune, or one God with three personalities. (The Amish view of the Trinity might best be called "Psychological Trinitarianism" as opposed to "Social Trinitarianism.") To me, I could never get used to the idea that God had "multiple personalities," as it were. Most of my Amish family and friends believed this, but the idea just didn't resonate with me. Something about it seemed amiss.

Another thing I never understood was why God would have prophets in biblical times but not have them in modern times. It seemed to me that the need for someone like a prophet was greater in our day than it was in biblical times. So why would God abandon us today, leaving us without the guidance we needed—without the guidance He seemed so willing to give in biblical times?

That being said, most everything else taught by the Amish I agreed with; and what I didn't agree with I just tried to force to the back of my mind. But I did still have the lingering concern about something my grandfather had frequently told me. He said, "The Amish Church is the *most true* Church." That always bothered me. Why did he not say that it was *the* "true Church"? As a consequence of his words, I believed for many years that the true Church was no longer on the earth and that we had just a reflection of the truth. I figured that there wasn't much we could do about that, but it still seemed bothersome.

Much of my teenage years were spent working the farm,

WHEN I LEFT THE **AMISH COMMUNITY** FOR THE FIRST TIME, I FULLY EXPECTED TO SEE **ROBOTS** THAT LOOKED LIKE PEOPLE WALKING THE STREETS.

going to school, and studying the Bible and other books. What most of the English don't realize is that the Amish *can* study things other than the Bible. Indeed, they are allowed to read almost anything they want, so long as it isn't immoral or pornographic. I personally loved studying history, economics, and, as a sideline hobby, science fiction. (I'm embarrassed to say that reading science fiction as an Amish kid actually caused me a bit of a problem in adulthood. When I left the Amish community for the first time, I fully expected to see robots that looked like people walking the streets.)

Many Amish leave home for a short period, sometime before their eighteenth birthday. You see, the Amish grew out of the sixteenth century Anabaptist movement, which taught that one should only baptize adults—*never children*. Because of this view on adult-baptism, it is common for Amish youth to participate in a rite of passage known as *rumspringa* (which literally means "running around"—but might best be called "sowing your wild oats").

During rumspringa, an Amish youth goes out in the world to see what is there—to learn about how the English live—with the intent of being able to make an informed decision as to whether they want to come back to the community and be baptized a member of the Amish faith. Having seen what's in the world, the young man or woman can then say with confidence, "I'm rejecting what the English do, and I want to live the lifestyle and faith of my childhood."

Some Amish youth in their late-adolescence use rumspringa mostly as an opportunity to look and observe how the rest of the world live. Some, on the other hand, engage in pretty rebellious behavior (for example, rejection of the traditional clothing and hair styles, driving vehicles, not tending to prayers, using alcohol or recreational drugs, defying parental norms, and even immorality—though certainly never anything as serious as murder). Again, this rite of passage simply allows the person participating to fully understand what the world has to offer and, therefore, allows the young man or woman to be able to make an informed choice about baptism and the Amish way.

When I was finally old enough to be baptized, I personally didn't see the point of participating in rumspringa, as I had already determined that I didn't want anything that the English had to offer. Three of my brothers, however, did participate; but they never shared their experiences of their time away from the community. Generally speaking, that's simply something one doesn't discuss when one returns home from rumspringa.

As was common among the Amish, I only attended school up until the eighth grade. I joined the Amish Church and was baptized shortly after my eighteenth birthday and, not too long after that, I married my wife. My baptism consisted of sitting in front of the congregation (which is called a "district") with the bishop standing behind me with his hands cupped above my head. The deacon then would pour water into the bishop's hands, and he would pour the water on my head three times, baptizing me in the name of the Father, and the Son, and the Holy Spirit.

It should be noted that, among the Amish, there are no church buildings. Church is held in the members' homes. Every year, one Amish family is given the opportunity to host church every other week. The off weeks, when there is no church, we are expected to go visit the sick, the elderly, and so on.

IF YOU ARE INTERESTED IN A GIRL, YOU CAN GIVE HER **A RIDE HOME** FROM CHURCH IN YOUR **BUGGY.**

Dating among the Amish is nothing like dating among the English.

Back home, if you are interested in a girl, you can give her a ride home from church in your buggy (with her father's permission, of course). After a couple of months of "dating by buggy," you can expect to get invited to the girl's house, where you'll sit silently in the front room while you listen to her family talk. Frankly, it's pretty boring, but you're traditionally not allowed to engage in conversation until you are part of the family.

After we were married, my wife and I spent the next week or so going to visit friends and relatives, and collecting our wedding presents. After that, there was a big celebration, and a sort of "barn raising." An Amish "barn raising" is when the community gets together to build a house and/ or a barn for the newly married couple. It is a real advantage that the Amish have over the English because the newly married Amish couples don't start off their marriage in debt; everyone starts with a nice house and barn.

I really loved my wife, and we had a great marriage. We were blessed with two wonderful daughters. It was interesting to me to see the changes in me as my daughters grew up. I had never been a very serious person. However, when my daughters were born, I felt a great responsibility toward them, both physically and spiritually. I believed, and still do, that someday I will stand before God and I will have to answer for the things that I taught (or didn't teach) them. Consequently, I tried very hard to fulfill my responsibilities as a father.

My life and marriage were pretty good for many years. Much of the doubt of my youth was assuaged by time and age and work, work, work.

Life went along in this fashion until approximately 2005, when my wife began complaining that she felt tired all of the time. In addition, she had some discomfort in her breasts. Sadly, we ignored these early signs. (What I wouldn't do to reverse that decision.) These symptoms continued until 2007. In February of that year, Opa passed away. This was particularly hard for me, as he and I had a special relationship—I being his namesake. Two months later, in April 2007, my mother woke up to find my father on the floor from an apparent stroke. He passed away the next day. My mother was especially devastated.

One night, after paying a visit to my widowed mother, I had a dream in which I saw my deceased father. He was dressed entirely in white, and asked me to let my mother know he was okay. This brought *some* comfort to her, but she was still in a lot of distress over his passing. In August of that year, Mother passed away—we assume because of a broken heart. (She greatly missed my father.) It was beginning to shape up to be a very bad year.

Not too long after Mother passed, my wife and I decided that a medical doctor should check out her continuing fatigue and pain. After a series of tests, we were informed that my wife had breast cancer, and that it was in stage IV. Further, we were told that there was basically nothing that could be done, as it had spread beyond the breast. We were grateful to finally know what was causing her symptoms, but we were devastated by the news that there was nothing we could do—and that death was just a matter of time. On December 23, 2007—my birthday—my dear wife passed away. Thank goodness 2007 was almost over, as I am not certain that I could have taken much more after the loss of my opa, father, mother, and wife.

Though I was unaware of it, during all of the family crises of that year, my eldest daughter was becoming quite serious with a certain young man. In January 2008, her would-be suitor paid me a visit to ask me for my daughter's hand. I was shocked, to say the least. This was the one time in my life when I was absolutely speechless. I said a quick prayer, and the thought came to me to relate to him a story from the Old Testament. The story was about Jacob, and how he wanted to marry Rachel (see Genesis 29). As the story goes, Jacob had to work for fourteen years to marry the woman that he loved. I suggested that this was proof of his commitment, and I wanted to know if this young man was as committed to my daughter as Jacob was to Rachel. After a rather long discussion with him, I felt convinced that this young man was indeed devoted to my daughter. I felt blessed that God had told me what to say to this young man, both to let him know what I expected but also to assure me that he would take care of my little girl. I often think back to moments in my life, such as this one, and recognize that they are evidence of the reality that there is a God who knows and loves me.

THEY ARE EVIDENCE OF THE **REALITY** THAT THERE IS A **GOD** WHO **KNOWS AND LOVES** ME.

Not too long after this, the Amish bishop approached me. He wanted to make me aware that there was a young woman in the district who was being supported by the community because of the passing of her husband. The bishop thought that it would be best for the community if I, as a widower, were to take on that responsibility. I am frank to say that it astounded me that he would think that I could (or should) marry a woman that I didn't love. What's more, I really believed in the concept of self-determination and felt that something of such great importance *absolutely* had to be my decision, and my decision alone.

In the ensuing months, the bishop and some of the elders from my district continued to make similar life-altering decisions on my behalf, and this caused me a great deal of consternation. As a result, the idea slowly began to formulate in my head that I had but one choice—to leave home and go live among the English. This was not an easy or *comfortable* decision for me, but—the more I entertained the idea and thought out the details of how I would accomplish this—I began

I HAD BUT ONE CHOICE—TO LEAVE HOME AND GO LIVE AMONG THE ENGLISH.

to realize that this was something that I was supposed to do. It seemed that God was directing my path.

I had been doing quite a lot of praying during this time, and one particular night—after a very earnest prayer—I had one of the most peaceful feelings I have ever had in my life. That confirmed to me that the decision I had made to leave the Amish community was the right one. At the same time, I also began having really sad feelings, both from the standpoint of leaving home, but also leaving my daughters with relatives. I was also overwhelmed with a sense of grief over the recent deaths of my loved ones.

After disposing of my belongings, I had my English friend, Jon, from Cincinnati come pick me up. I had known Jon for many years, as he would hire many in our community to do carpentry work for him on various projects he was spearheading. When he learned that I was leaving home, Jon had insisted that I come to live with him, and he took it upon himself to "educate" me. This "education" consisted mainly of watching movies together and him making fun of the way I talked, of my perception of reality, and how I looked. I believe he meant this in the best possible way, and as a means of helping me to become more acclimated to English society. One would think that getting repeatedly teased for being "different" would be offensive, but, owing to my love for laughter, it really only served to endear Jon to me.

Over the span of almost five years, Jon and I spent just about every waking moment together. In addition to our movie-watching, we went to a lot of construction sites, and we did a lot of volunteer work for neighbors and friends—which I absolutely loved!

I learned a lot from Jon, particularly how to act English. At first, I had to develop the skill of acting like I knew what people were talking about—even when I had no background or experience from which to draw. This was especially true when speaking of television programs. Having grown up *never* watching TV, I didn't recognize *any* of the shows people referenced and, so, I just became really good at pretending. I was only caught in my charade once. I had made some random remark, and Jon turned, looked at me, and said, "You don't have the foggiest idea of what we're saying, do you?"

Jon became a close and trusted friend. Thus, I was devastated to learn (in 2012) that he had been diagnosed with cancer that, by the time of its discovery, was widespread. As was his nature, he took the news in a spirit of optimism and levity, saying, "Well, now I can take up smoking!" Jon passed away on my birthday, December 23, 2012. Needless to say, I don't like my birthday much anymore.

NEEDLESS TO SAY, **I DON'T LIKE MY BIRTHDAY** MUCH ANYMORE.

Once again, I was faced with a dilemma: Where to go?

Jon and I had always discussed the west, specifically Utah, because of the mountains, the camping, the hiking, and so forth. Having nowhere else to go, I decided that since we had always talked about visiting Utah, that was the place to go. One fine Saturday morning in February 2013, I went to downtown Cincinnati, purchased a bus ticket to Salt Lake City, and turned my attention toward Utah. It was all quite scary for me, knowing no one and sitting in a bus terminal among some very "interesting" people. Eventually the bus started loading, and I was on my way!

Where would I stay when I arrived in Salt Lake? I really had no plan. And, while I had not thought through the details, finding housing would be more complex than I had anticipated, particularly since I had no identification and no birth certificate. This is actually a common problem for any who leave the Amish faith. When an English baby is born, they are typically born in a hospital, or under a doctor's care. Back home, about half of the Amish are born in their homes. Consequently, a significant number do not have birth certificates or driver's licenses either, since they're not needed to drive a horse and buggy. So, we are often undocumented—and that makes for an interesting adventure when one tries to become part of mainstream America.

After talking with various people that I had met en route to Utah, I learned about the website craigslist.com. Using that, I began working on finding a place to stay when I arrived in Salt Lake City.

I located a man on the Internet who lived on the east side of downtown Salt Lake and who was looking for a roommate to share housing expenses. That sounded good to me, so I made the arrangements, and now had a place to stay when I actually arrived.

Our bus route brought us up through St. George, and then north through the heart of Utah. In St. George, on a hill behind the bus stop, I saw a most beautiful building. A little twenty-year-old, who had gotten on the bus in Arizona, informed me that it was the Mormon temple. I generally knew who the Mormons were, but had no idea what the temple was for. I assumed it was probably a building for Sunday church services.

On traveling north, through Payson, Utah, we saw another Mormon temple under construction. Again, quite beautiful!

I arrived in Salt Lake City in the late afternoon, and took a taxi to my new home in the avenues. As I toured the house I had planned on living in, it was apparent that I couldn't stay there. It was quite filthy and infested with cockroaches. Old food, dirty dinner plates, trash, and soiled clothes littered nearly every square inch of the house. The living conditions were abhorrent.

This presented a bit of a dilemma. It was early evening and I had no place to spend the night. Without any identification, I couldn't rent a motel room, and even the homeless shelter wouldn't let me stay there without ID. I had not slept the previous night, and so I was quite tired. But I decided

IT WAS APPARENT THAT I COULDN'T STAY THERE. IT WAS QUITE FILTHY AND INFESTED WITH COCKROACHES.

I would just walk around downtown Salt Lake until morning. I would make living arrangements that next day.

As I began walking around in the cool of the night, I saw a building that drew my attention. I later learned that it was yet another Mormon temple, and I was generally pleased with the appearance of the downtown area. I started to get a little hungry, so I went into a hotel to inquire as to whether there were any all-night restaurants close by. As I explained my situation to the hotel clerk, he gave me a little map to a Denny's restaurant just down the street. What I didn't realize was that a young man sitting in the hotel lobby was listening to my conversation with the clerk.

It was now about 1:30 a.m., and I was still quite hungry. As I headed out of the hotel, the young man from the lobby followed me and, catching up to me, said, "Hey, I can rent you a hotel room if you need me to, and you can just pay me for it and give me a couple of bucks for the trouble." This sounded really good to me, and almost seemed like a miracle, so I readily agreed. As we started walking down the street toward a motel, he said, "Better yet, you can just come sleep on my couch and give me like twenty dollars." This sounded even better, since it would save me some money. (Yes, I'm a cheapskate.)

Following him down the street turned out to be somewhat difficult. He was quite tall and his stride quite long—and I was tired from having walked around all day—but I managed to keep up. As we approached an old, run-down apartment building, he said, "This is where my girl-friend used to live, and I still have the key." This seemed odd to me, but I followed him in, and we headed down a dark hallway. Suddenly, he walked back toward the front of the building and proceeded to run up the stairs, saying, "Wait here, I'll be right back!" His behavior was quite puzzling to me. Suddenly, a voice within me said as clear as could be, that I needed to get out of there, and

SUDDENLY, **A VOICE WITHIN ME** SAID AS CLEAR AS COULD BE, THAT I NEEDED TO **GET OUT OF THERE**, AND GET OUT OF THERE NOW.

get out of there now. I hesitated for a second, and then it came again, "Run!" So, I ran . . . and I ran . . . and I ran.

14

After about ten minutes of running as hard as I could, I was back in the downtown area and near the Denny's restaurant I was originally looking for.

As I've thought about the events of that night, I know that God—through the Holy Ghost—was watching over and protecting me.

The next day I looked back on Craigslist for a place to stay. I quickly found a suitable place in Draper, Utah—just south of Salt Lake City. The young man who had posted the add showed me the lodgings and, after hearing my story, agreed that he would rent me his place. He indicated that it would be available in two days. Two days? What was I supposed to do for the next two days? I asked if I could move in right away, explaining that I needed somewhere to stay, and that I had no way to rent a hotel room. Feeling my desperation, and a sense of concern for me, he indicated that his father owned a house in Cottonwood Heights (southeast of Salt Lake) and that he had a few rooms available there. He was kind enough to give me a ride so that I could look at the rental. As we drove, this young man told me about the Mormon Church and indicated that he had once been a missionary for that Church. We eventually reached the house and inspected the facility, which proved to be quite adequate.

SINCE I HAD NOTHING BETTER TO DO, I READ IT IN ITS ENTIRETY IN THREE DAYS.

As we were parting ways, he asked me if I would do him a favor. I agreed, wondering what on earth he could ask of me, a complete stranger? He gave me a copy of the Book of Mormon, and asked if I would read it. I agreed to and, since I had nothing better to do, I read it in its entirety in three days.

Much to my surprise, about three weeks later, two young girls appeared at the door. I answered the knock (this was before I knew not to answer the door when someone knocks!), and they asked for one of my roommates. I later learned that these young girls were missionaries from the LDS Church. When I informed them that he wasn't there, they asked me if I had heard of the Mormon Church. I told them I had been hearing of nothing but the Mormon Church for a while now and that I had read the Book of Mormon. At this point, I saw the dollar signs light up in their eyes, and they asked if they could start teaching me about the Church. I agreed. (Again, more joy filled their countenances!)

As they taught me about The Church of Jesus Christ of Latter-day Saints, everything they said I already believed. None of the doctrine was objectionable to me. I did have a problem, however, with being taught by women—especially *young* women—and I let them know that. (In the Amish faith, women don't teach the men. It just isn't done.) Nevertheless, these sister missionaries kept coming every week, and every week they would say, "Will you be baptized on Saturday?" And every week I would say, "No." My repeated rejections of their invitations wasn't because I didn't believe what they were teaching me, but because they continually asked me, even after I had said "No." I guess the Amish in me makes me a little stubborn. In point of fact, I knew when I first read the Book of Mormon that it was absolutely true and that the Mormon Church was true. I had read the book, prayed about the book, and received a definite answer from God that it was true. My father and grandfather had both instilled in me a belief that I was able to feel the truth of most things. They told me that this was a gift God had given to me, and I believe that even now. Thus, I *knew!*

MY **REPEATED REJECTIONS** OF THEIR INVITATIONS WASN'T BECAUSE I DIDN'T BELIEVE WHAT THEY WERE TEACHING ME, BUT BECAUSE **THEY CONTINUALLY ASKED ME, EVEN AFTER I HAD SAID "NO."**

This process of visiting with the missionaries, attending church, being taught, being invited to be baptized, and rejecting that invitation went on for almost a year, and eight or nine different missionaries cycled through my home and my life. I can't say for certain all that kept me from committing, but clearly my Amish culture was a great stumbling block in my efforts to live what I knew to be right and true.

One Sunday, a member of the stake high council asked if I would meet with him and the missionaries after Church. I agreed. We met in one of the small classrooms there in the church building, and I knew—even before we began—that the conversation was going to revolve around me joining the Mormon Church. As we entered the room, I decided that I would take charge. So, I rather abruptly said, "Well, I should probably tell the three of you that I have decided to join the Mormon Church." Shocked doesn't begin to describe the expression on their faces. But there were also a lot of happy looks too.

There is a statement (perhaps apocryphal) that has been attributed to Brigham Young, in which he says that, after his conversion, it took years to get the Methodist out of him. I can certainly relate to that. Since my conversion, I've often referred to myself as "Mormonish." While I am firmly in the faith, my Amish background will always color who I am and how I think. Was my decision to finally get baptized a result of me getting over my Amish cultural issues, or because of something else? I really don't know. But I knew the time was right to act on what the Spirit had revealed to me nearly a year previous. I was baptized a member of The Church of Jesus Christ of Latter-day Saints on February 1, 2013, and I received my endowment in the holy temple on August 29, 2014.

Throughout this process, I have learned that God knows and loves me. And even though I am as imperfect a human being as exists on this planet, I have felt that He knows what's happening in my life, and He actually cares what happens to me. Though I have no contact with my two daughters, my siblings, or other family members—I've been shunned and, therefore, contact is impossible—I know that God will arrange things for me to be reunited someday with my family—whether in time or in eternity. Meanwhile, my faith in the restored gospel gives me purpose and the power to endure. For this, I am so very grateful to God.

ABE

A LESSON TO BE LEARNED

Abe's conversion reminds me of a principle taught by the Prophet Joseph Smith. He once said, "To become a joint heir of the heirship of the Son, one must put away all his false traditions."[1] George Q. Cannon, a counselor in the First Presidency to four presidents of the Church, noted his personal frustration with the fact that the people were "so slow" to "comprehend things and so enshrouded in . . . ignorant traditions" that he worried that the Prophet Joseph, "With the knowledge he possessed and the progress he had made could not stay with the people." Because they allowed their "ignorant traditions" to cloud their ability to see the truth, Cannon feared God would simply take the prophet out of the people's midst.[2]

Certainly some traditions are good and helpful: holiday traditions, family traditions, traditions utilized to commemorate a sacred event or rite of passage. However, time and again, the scriptures condemn "the traditions of their fathers, which are not correct" (Mosiah 1:5; see also Galatians 1:14; Alma 9:17; Helaman 15:15; D&C 74:4). If our traditions prevent us from seeing truth, they will serve as a stumbling block rather than a blessing. I have known quite a few people who have investigated the Church and received a witness through the Holy Ghost that it is true—but, because their conversion would upset the proverbial "apple cart," they would not join. They placed the "traditions of their fathers" before the dictates of their God; and the consequence was a loss of blessings for them and their posterity.

May we have the courage to look beyond our traditions and, where necessary, set them aside so that we will be recipients of the tremendous blessings God has in store.

ALONZO

NOTES

1. *Teachings of the Prophet Joseph Smith*, comp. Joseph Fielding Smith Jr. (1924), 321.

2. "Discourse by President George Q. Cannon," *Millennial Star* 61, no. 40 (October 5, 1899): 629.

ATHEIST

DANIEL ORTNER

I was born in Tel Aviv, Israel. My parents moved to Florida when I was about three and a half. I was raised in a Jewish household in which Judaism played a large role culturally, but a rather small role spiritually. We would go to synagogue for the High Holiday services, and then go back home and eat shrimp and pork—two things practicing Jews are forbidden to eat (see Leviticus 11:7–8, 10). My father was a very secular individual, and his lack of belief in God was rooted in the gas chambers of Auschwitz and multiplied by heartbreak and loss throughout his life. If there was a God in heaven, how could He allow such things to happen?

My mother was the more spiritual of the two. She taught me to believe in God and to love that which is spiritual. And yet, she also believed in a God that did not know or care about the little things that we did. "God doesn't have an IBM computer," she would remind me whenever I would ask why we

WE WOULD GO TO SYNAGOGUE FOR THE HIGH HOLIDAY SERVICES, AND THEN GO BACK HOME AND EAT SHRIMP AND PORK.

didn't keep the same commandments my orthodox friends did. In other words, God isn't keeping track of who keeps the commandments and who doesn't. And yet, for all of their laxness, my parents sent me to a Jewish private elementary school and had my Bar Mitzvah—the traditional Jewish rite of passage into adulthood—at the age of thirteen. Still, religion was not a very large part of my life.

Nonetheless, I had a lot of experiences that led me to wonder about the purpose of life. I remember as a small child asking my mother what happened after death, and she didn't really have a response. She said she hoped there was something after this life, but she wasn't entirely sure. I went to the library and read books (written for kids) about death, but, again, I didn't find any answers there either. My grandfather died when I was six, and my grandmother when I was eight. Death seemed like an awful force that I could not fully understand, but which I feared.

As I got older, my father—who had long suffered from heart problems—began to have serious health issues. Late one night, when I was in fifth grade, he had to be taken to the hospital by ambulance. Then, when I was eleven years old, he had his third open-heart surgery. The possibility of his death was ever present in my mind.

In the midst of all of this turmoil, I continued to search for spiritual answers that would help me understand why people die, what happens when they do, and why there is so much suffering in the world. After elementary school, I stopped attending the

> **DEATH** SEEMED LIKE AN **AWFUL FORCE** THAT I COULD NOT FULLY UNDERSTAND, BUT WHICH I **FEARED.**

Jewish private school, and went to a public middle and high school. There, for the first time, I was surrounded by people of other faiths, and I began to take an interest in Christianity.

One of my best friends at the time was a strong believer in Christ, and she really helped me to learn more about Him. She had a light about her and, despite my life that was so filled with darkness and trials, I was drawn to that special light that she had. She prayed for me, asking God that I would always be surrounded by strong Christian acquaintances and, in many ways, that prayer was answered. It seemed that, wherever I traveled and however far I moved away from God, people of faith seemed to be placed in my path. Thanks to her influence, and that of several others, I began more and more to believe in Jesus Christ. In addition to the influence of good friends, I also had a number of experiences—such spiritually significant dreams—that led me to believe in a God and in Jesus Christ. I remember reading Isaiah 53 and trembling with awe at the description of the Lamb of God suffering for the sins of all mankind.

And yet, something held me back from fully committing to Christ. In part, it was the opposition of my parents, whose hearts broke when I told them about my interest in Christianity. In addition, I still had several nagging questions that I just did not feel were settled. I wondered what would happen to the generations of my ancestors who had lived and died Jewish. They had faced the gas chambers and pogroms because of their faith. I could not accept the notion of a God that would condemn them to hell, and yet my Christian friends offered little hope. Consequently, I began to slowly drift away from Christianity

When I was fifteen years old, my mom was diagnosed with ovarian cancer. It came as a total shock to me, because she had always been the healthier of my parents. We both believed strongly that God would deliver her. But, even though she fought valiantly, she died shortly after my eighteenth birthday. Her last months of life were especially difficult, even though her faith in the face of that trial was inspiring. The loss was

> THEY HAD **FACED THE GAS CHAMBERS** AND POGROMS BECAUSE OF THEIR FAITH. I **COULD NOT ACCEPT** THE NOTION OF **A GOD THAT WOULD CONDEMN THEM TO HELL.**

absolutely devastating to me and, in time, it continued to gnaw away at my faith. As I began my undergraduate studies at Brandeis University, I began to read the writings of the famed atheists, Richard Dawkins and Christopher Hitchens, and I quickly fell under their spell. I didn't know how to accept a God that would allow my mother to suffer, and so I went to the opposite extreme—denying His existence.

My atheism was predicated on three foundational pillars: first, that God was highly improbable; second, that belief in God was a force for evil or harm in the world; and third, that I did not need or want faith in God because I could be a good person without such faith.

In time, I became deeply involved in the secular humanist community in the Boston area. I became a founding member of the Brandeis Humanists and attended debates, speaker events, and meetings. I believed that I had been enlightened, freed from an ignorant and superstitious belief in God. I felt it my mission to help others to see the light.

> I BELIEVED THAT I HAD BEEN ENLIGHTENED, **FREED FROM AN IGNORANT** AND **SUPER-STITIOUS BELIEF IN GOD.**

Around this time, I became friends with a girl named Tatiana, whom I later discovered was Mormon. She was one of the only two undergraduate members of the LDS Church in the whole of Brandeis University! She wasn't active in the Church at the time, but she still held many of the values common to Latter-day Saints. She wouldn't drink and had a very traditional view about the role of women—which stood out in a very "progressive," feminist-friendly university like Brandeis. I became really intrigued by her values.

At the end of my sophomore year at Brandeis, I had several experiences that made me realize I was not becoming the person that I wanted to be. I felt powerless to change and improve myself. And, when I experienced a particularly difficult break up with my girlfriend, I realized that I did not have a firm foundation of belief to fall back on. One of the pillars upon which I had built my atheism, namely my belief that I did not need God in my life, suddenly began to crumble.

That summer, I studied abroad in China and, while there, had an instructor who was a strong member of the local Christian community. We had numerous conversations about God and religion, and those lengthy discussions began to open my mind up to the possibility that there could be a God. As I observed his vibrant spirituality, the second pillar of my atheism—my belief that faith was a force for evil—now began to weaken. I began to yearn for something more in my life, and I began to sense that religion might be the thing to satisfy that yearning.

When I returned to Boston, I learned that Tatiana had decided to begin going back to church. As a result of the experiences that I had that summer, I felt prompted to look into her Church. Up to that point I knew next to nothing about Mormonism, aside from what I had seen on *South Park*, of course. So I went to Barnes and Noble, picked up *Mormonism for*

Dummies[1] and *The Complete Idiot's Guide to Understanding Mormonism*,[2] sat down, and began to read. As I read, I was really struck by the power of the doctrine. I began to read about the pre-earth life, the plan of salvation, and the postmortal spirit world—and these doctrines just felt right. What I was discovering filled a hole in my soul. It all immediately made sense to me. It answered the various questions I'd had about how one could believe Christ was the way and yet also believe that those who didn't know Him could be saved. I went to my friend Tatiana and asked her if I could go to church with her.

The next day, which was Sunday, she and I attended the Cambridge University Ward. We were late for sacrament meeting, so I ended up going only to Sunday School and Priesthood, but what struck me was how friendly people were. Tatiana had encouraged me to wear a suit and tie, so people assumed that I was a member of the Church. I was actually asked to give a closing prayer in one of the meetings. When I indicated that I wasn't actually a member of the Church, I could tell by the look on people's faces that they were a bit surprised. As would be expected, when people discovered a "nonmember" in their midst, they quickly arranged for me to meet the missionaries.

In anticipation of meeting with the elders, I made a mental list of a whole bunch of questions I had relating to the doctrines of the Church. I peppered them with some pretty difficult ones, such as, "Why are there transgender and hermaphroditic individuals if gender is a premortal trait?" and "What happens to those that have more than one husband or wife in this life?" I have to hand it to them. The poor missionaries did a great job of deflecting the controversial questions and inviting me to sincerely read and pray.

Even at that early point in my investigation of the Church, I knew I was feeling something special. I told my friend Tatiana that she shouldn't expect me to be baptized quickly or anything, but that I could really see myself liking the LDS Church. I had some hangups with the Church's conservative

I CONTINUED TO **READ EVERYTHING** I COULD FIND ABOUT THE CHURCH— **BOTH PRO- AND ANTI-MORMON SOURCES**—AND I FELT **DRAWN** MORE AND MORE **TO THE CHURCH.**

political position on things like gay marriage. However, I continued to read everything I could find about the Church—both pro- and anti-Mormon sources—and I felt drawn more and more to the Church.

One day I was talking to a nonmember friend who is really opposed to Mormonism. She began to bash the Church, and she was especially vitriolic regarding the LDS temple. She had a good friend that was married in the temple and that friend's family could not attend the wedding since they were not members. My friend was absolutely disgusted by this practice. As she spoke to me, I was pretty taken aback and wondered why that was the policy. While thinking about it, I felt strongly prompted to go visit the Boston LDS temple. Though it was 9 p.m., I got into my car and drove to the temple grounds.

As I got out of my car, I felt an overwhelming spiritual presence. I had never felt anything quite so powerful. I felt it through every fiber of my being. I felt as if God was present and was talking directly to me. In my mind, I heard His voice telling me that the Church was true and that He was there. I was stubborn, and so I got back into my car and I drove to the nearby Catholic and Protestant churches to see if I would feel the same way there. I didn't feel anything of the sort—in fact, I felt quite the opposite. I then got back into my car and drove back to the temple. I went to a fairly secluded spot and knelt down in front of one of the stained glass windows. There, I poured my heart out to God, and I felt transformed by the Spirit. The final pillar of my atheism—my belief that I did not need God—definitively shattered. My whole being was filled with light. In that moment, I could clearly see the person that the Lord wanted me to become. I could see my potential as His son. I knew without a doubt that God loved me and wanted me to join His Church. I knew that I should be baptized. In a sense, the words of Alma seemed written for me: "Blessed is he that believeth in the word of God, and is baptized without stubbornness of heart" (Alma 32:16). Since that moment, I have never doubted the truthfulness of the Gospel. Even in my darkest moments, that experience has been like a beacon of light.

THE **FINAL PILLAR OF MY ATHEISM**—MY BELIEF THAT I DID NOT NEED GOD—**DEFINITIVELY SHATTERED.**

Telling my father about my decision to be baptized was not at all an easy thing to do. Not long after this spiritual experience at the temple, we met in New York for the Jewish High Holidays. The weekend before, I had been with my ward in Sharon, Vermont, at the site of Joseph Smith's birthplace. There I had borne my testimony that I knew the Church was true. One week later, sharing with my father that same testimony was much more difficult.

We walked near Lincoln Center, with the Manhattan temple nearby, and I finally worked up the courage to tell him. His reaction was, of course, quite negative—as I would have expected. He strongly forbade me from getting baptized and told me that, if I did, he would want nothing to do with me. In an effort to calm him, I compromised with my father, and agreed that I would wait six months before being baptized. I thought that would help him to see that this was the sincere desire of my heart.

I spent the next semester studying abroad in London, and it was a pretty challenging time in many ways. Throughout it all, however, I went to church every Sunday and bore my testimony each month during fast and testimony meeting. At times, I felt quite alone; but my faith in the Atonement of Christ got me through the difficult days.

After six months, my father was still as opposed as ever to my being baptized and, so, as painful as it was, I postponed my baptism *again*. Even though I was legally an adult, my father's approval was ultimately very important to me, and I wanted to show him that I respected him. I was about to leave Florida to drive up to Philadelphia for the summer, when my father finally gave me his permission to be baptized. Alma's words suddenly took on new meaning for me: "I have been supported under trials and troubles of every kind, yea, and in all manner of afflictions" (Alma 36:27). God had intervened, and I felt so very blessed. I went up to Boston the next weekend and was baptized in the University Ward there. I still remember the joy that I felt when I was baptized. I felt cleansed from all of my sins, and I felt like an innocent child in the eyes of God. It was such a wonderful and unforgettable feeling.

Although there were challenges after my baptism and confirmation, I felt a new energy and ability to cope with those trials. My coworkers that summer were strongly critical of the Church because of its stance on this or that, and I struggled with internal doubts over some of those same topics, but I kept on striving and struggling.

Not too long after my baptism, my ward made a trip to Palmyra. While there, I took the opportunity to pray in the Sacred Grove and felt the Lord confirm to me once again that *everything* I had come to believe was true. That summer was one of great growth and development; and, as a bonus, I met my future wife while living in Philadelphia!

Still, one of the hardest decisions loomed before me. Even before baptism, I had begun wondering whether I would have to serve a mission. I began rationalizing and telling myself that, since I was older than most missionaries, I wouldn't have to do so. Nevertheless, I felt really strongly that I *should* serve, and that that service would transform my life for the better in so many ways. It was ultimately a difficult choice knowing how strong my father's opposition would be. However, I realized that whenever I thought about serving, I felt incredible peace and calm, while when I thought about staying home, I felt selfish and ill at ease. I felt a burning desire to share the gospel with others and to help them feel what I felt. Ultimately, I knew that I *had to* serve. I filled out my papers, deferred from law school, and told my father about my decision to serve a mission.

Of course, he didn't take that well and, once again, he threatened to disown me. The hardest part wasn't the threat. Rather, it was seeing the pain that I knew I was causing him. Yet I understood that serving would ultimately secure for me an eternal family. Still, I remember feeling so physically

ULTIMATELY, I KNEW THAT I HAD TO SERVE.

and spiritually ill when I put in my papers. I had to remember to "cast not away my confidence" and to rely on the Lord (see Hebrews 10:35). For weeks I felt discomforted and filled with despair. I was certain I'd never see my father again if I served a mission. I didn't know how I would pay for schooling once I got back. Yet I put my faith in the Lord. When I got my call and heard that I would be serving in Novosibirsk, Russia, I felt the Spirit fill me with an overwhelming sense of peace and a confirmation that what I was doing was right.

I had the most incredible mission experience. I loved serving the Lord, and I am so grateful for that experience. I know that the call was inspired of God. On my mission, I gained a far deeper testimony of the Savior and His Church. I came to know Him as I learned to love and serve His children. Since then, I have graduated law school (from BYU) and married, and we have two beautiful daughters.

Perhaps most important of all, my testimony is still burning strong, and I am filled with conviction and with the power of the Lord. I am so grateful to Him for the tremendous blessings He has given me, and for the opportunities that yet lay ahead.

DANIEL

A LESSON TO BE LEARNED

In the Book of Mormon, Nephi's brother, Jacob, warns us: "O the vainness, and the frailties, and the foolishness of men! When they are learned they think they are wise, . . . supposing they know of themselves, wherefore, their wisdom is foolishness and it profiteth them not. . . . But to be learned is good if they hearken unto the counsels of God" (2 Nephi 9:28–29).

The mind is an amazing thing. What humankind has discovered, invented, and imagined over the millennia is truly mindboggling. Of course, there is always the danger of thinking—because humans have accomplished *so much*—that the creature is as worthy of adulation as the Creator. Such a thought, if left unchecked, will at best lead to secular humanism and, at worst, atheism.

A close friend of mine, formerly an atheist, recently confided to me,

> As an atheist, I too had to be a man of faith. I exercised faith in many scientific theories that I could not personally prove to be true, but which I simply trusted were. I exercised faith in the proposition that if the big bang theory were true, then there could not be a God. At one point it just struck me: why couldn't there be a God who created through physics—even through the big bang? Why not believe equally as hard in a physicist God as in no God at all? Then, next thing I knew, I had converted—and had not really had to throw out much of what I believed.

The mind is a wonderful thing; and it will serve us best when we realize that everything we know—science, religion, relationships, etc.—is all a matter of faith. When we come to that realization, true conversion can take place.

ALONZO

NOTES

1. Jana Riess and Christopher Kimball Bigelow, *Mormonism for Dummies* (Hoboken, New Jersey: Wiley Publishing, Inc., 2005).

2. Drew Williams, *The Complete Idiot's Guide to Understanding Mormonism* (New York: Penguin, 2003).

BAPTIST

BRYAN READY

I t just wouldn't leave me alone." That's the answer I usually give when people ask me why I became a member of The Church of Jesus Christ of Latter-day Saints. For me, it wasn't about a search for truth or a powerful testimony that I heard someone bear. Rather, my conversion came because of a strange, spiritual "pull" that just wouldn't go away.

I suppose it all started when I was about ten years old. It was 1979, and I was a huge fan of the Osmonds. ("Crazy Horses" is awesome!) That fall, an LDS friend had invited my mother and me to attend a "fireside" featuring the Osmond family and a professional baseball player named Harmon Killebrew. I remember sitting about halfway back in the cultural hall, listening to the Osmonds bear their testimonies. They talked about their faith in Jesus Christ, their belief in the restored gospel, and the miracles that they had experienced in their lives and career. I was as impressed as a ten-year-old could be.

On the way home, having mulled over in my mind what I had just experienced, I turned to my mother and said, "Mom, I want to be a Mormon." To which she responded, "We'll talk about this when we get home." When we arrived at the house her rather matter-of-fact answer was "No!"—and that was the end of it.

"MOM, I WANT TO BE A MORMON."

But a seed had been planted, a seed that would take some thirty-six years to bear fruit.

Over the next few years, my interactions with the LDS Church and its people were infrequent, with one exception—the Book of Mormon. You see, we had visited Temple Square on our family vacation a year or two after the Osmond fireside. At that time, you could buy a *Book of Mormon* for one dollar at the visitor's center. My mom bought a copy and kept it on her shelf. I'm not sure why. I didn't really ever see her read from it. But every once in a while I would pull it down and peruse its pages. I don't know if it was the attractive blue cover that drew me to the book, but something attracted me to it. I tried to read it, but, I must admit, it didn't make much sense to me; so I would thumb through the pages and look at the pictures. I did this quite a few times over the years.

That periodic "spiritual pull" returned when I was fourteen years old. I had grown up in a Christian home, where my parents sporadically attended a Presbyterian congregation—though we weren't "officially" members of any particular denomination. That year I was invited to attend a youth retreat at a nearby Southern Baptist Church. So far as I can recall, it was the first time I had stepped foot into a Baptist church. That Friday night we sang songs, played games, and had a Bible study. But the moment that changed my life forever was when the church's pastor taught us about Christ— about the Gospel or "good news" of Jesus. He pointed out how the scriptures say that we're all sinners (see Romans 6:23), and how Jesus suffered and died for our sins (see Romans 5:8; John 3:16). After he had preached what I thought was a pretty good sermon, he then invited each of us to place our faith and trust in Jesus Christ and to commit our lives to Him (see Romans 10:9). The pastor led us in what Evangelicals call "The Sinner's Prayer," which traditionally goes something like this: "Father in Heaven, I know that I am a sinner. I know that Jesus Christ suffered and died for my sins, that He paid the price for my sins. I know that Jesus is the Son of God. I want Him to come into my life. I repent of my sins and commit my life to You. In Jesus's Name, Amen." I can't recall

> THE **MOMENT** THAT **CHANGED** MY LIFE **FOREVER** WAS WHEN THE CHURCH'S **PASTOR TAUGHT** US **ABOUT CHRIST.**

if that is word for word what I prayed, but it captures the gist of what I said to God that day. I prayed that prayer and my life changed.

Now, let me be clear; there were no flashes of light—no theophany. I didn't see angels or hear God's voice. But my life changed for the better that night. I was different—a new person than I was when I arrived (see 2 Corinthians 5:17). Shortly thereafter, my mother and I joined that same Southern Baptist Church, and I would remain a member of it for the next thirty-three years. Nurtured by the Baptist Church, my faith in Christ grew quickly.

A few months later, I felt the "spiritual pull" once more. I was listening to late-night Christian talk radio and I heard the folks on the program talk about a new book that had just been released, titled *The God Makers*.[1] It was billed as an exposé that would inform its readers about what the Mormon Church "really" believes. That caught my attention. I remembered my encounter with the LDS faith a few years prior, and I decided to read the book.

The sensationalistic presentation of this anti-Mormon book really captured my imagination and, even though it was ardently critical of all things LDS, it reignited my fascination with Mormonism. Indeed, reading that book provoked in me an unquenchable desire to understand the Latter-day Saints, and it started my lifelong study of the LDS faith. Before long, I had subscribed to every anti-Mormon newsletter I could find, and I would take every opportunity I could to bash with those poor, young LDS missionaries who had the misfortune of knocking on my front door.

In time, I felt God calling me into the ministry, and so I decided to pursue a theological education. In 1990, I graduated from Union University in Jackson, Tennessee, with a BA in religion. I went on to earn two degrees at the Southern Baptist Theological Seminary, in Louisville, Kentucky—an MDiv in missions, evangelism, and church growth, and a ThM in world religions. Nearly every paper I wrote during my seminary training had something to do with the LDS faith— either explaining Baptist beliefs to the LDS people, or explaining how to

NEARLY EVERY PAPER I WROTE DURING MY SEMINARY TRAINING HAD SOMETHING TO DO WITH THE LDS FAITH.

evangelize the LDS people. I just couldn't let Mormonism go. It possessed me!

During this time, I served as a Minister of Music and Youth in churches in Illinois and Kentucky. However, sometime around the year 2000, I began to feel that God was calling me to be a pastor over a congregation, rather than just a youth minister. There was one slight problem with this—I didn't want to be a pastor. But, when God calls you to do something on His behalf, He is *relentless*. I realize we have our agency—and I certainly resisted that calling for a long time—but when God wants you to do something, He loves you enough to pursue you until you see that what He has planned for you is really what's best for you. So in December 2000, I became pastor of Mt. Zion Baptist Church in Piasa, Illinois. I would be their pastor for the next fifteen years. It was my first pastorate and, much to my surprise, my last. The folks at Mt. Zion were great Christian people. I grew to love them deeply, and they grew to love my family and me. Resigning as their pastor was one of the hardest things I've ever done.

Being a Baptist pastor didn't dampen my curiosity about all things Mormon. Having developed a passion for LDS history, I visited Mormon historic sites

BEING A **BAPTIST PASTOR** DIDN'T DAMPEN MY **CURIOSITY ABOUT ALL THINGS MORMON.**

whenever I had the chance. (Man, my wife is a saint for putting up with my weirdness all of those years!) Fortunately, Nauvoo, Illinois, is only about a three-hour drive from my house, so my family and I made frequent visits. Nauvoo has a special spirit about it—a feeling of peace that you don't experience in many places. I discovered that one of the best times to visit Nauvoo is in the summer, when the Nauvoo Pageant is taking place. It was during a 2011 Nauvoo Pageant performance that I was asked by some missionaries if I would like to have a CD of the pageant music. Well, I loved the pageant and so I signed up to receive a free CD. A few weeks later, two LDS missionaries—Elders Louk and Young, along with a local ward member, Brother Lynn Ennis—showed up at my door with the CD. Suddenly things in my life began to change *again*.

The four of us had a cordial conversation, and I received my free CD. As we finished our chat, one of the missionaries asked if they could come back and teach me a lesson the next week. I told them that I had gone through the missionary lessons many times before, and it probably wouldn't be a wise use of their time. But they were persistent, and so I relented, and we scheduled an appointment for the next week. When the lesson was over, one of the elders asked me if I had any questions. And then it just hit me: "Yes," I said, "I do have a question. I have been fascinated by the LDS Church, and have studied its doctrines and history intently for over thirty years, and I want to know why. Why has God allowed me to be so fixated on this faith? Has it all been a horrible waste of time, or does God have a purpose in all of this?" As you can imagine, this was not exactly the kind of question the elders thought they would be fielding.

"WHY HAS **GOD ALLOWED** ME TO BE SO **FIXATED** ON **THIS FAITH?"**

For the next year and a half, I met with the missionaries on a weekly basis. We studied every lesson more than once, and we even started studying the *Gospel Principles* manual. (They were desperate to find something to teach me that I had not already been taught.) The missionaries kept on me about praying about the things they were sharing with me and about setting a baptismal date. Eventually I felt that things were getting to the point that I needed to pray and specifically ask God if He wanted me to join the LDS Church. I'll never forget that moment. It was late at night, and I was kneeling by my bed. I asked the Lord if He wanted me to become a member of the LDS Church. Much to my surprise, the answer came very clearly, and very loudly: "NO!" I was taken aback. I thought for sure, given the way things had been progressing and owing to the positive feelings I had developed about the Church and its history, that the answer would be in the affirmative. As hard as I knew it would be for the missionaries to hear, at our next meeting I told them what I had experienced in answer to my prayer. Of course, they were disappointed; but we each felt prompted that we should continue meeting for the time being. It would be four more years before I understood why God had said "No" to my request to become a member of The Church of Jesus Christ of Latter-day Saints.

I continued to meet off and on with various sets of missionaries for the next four years. The mission president even visited me a few times. I had set more than one baptismal date, but each fell through as I struggled to know God's will for me. When various Latter-day Saints would ask me why I hadn't been baptized yet, I usually told them that it boiled down to three things—Jesus, Jennifer, and a job. Let me explain. After the firm "No" the Lord had given me the first time I prayed about joining the Church, I felt I needed an equally firm "Yes" before I could move forward and be baptized. In addition, I was still the pastor of a Baptist congregation. *My heavens!* How could I be baptized until I was "released" from that responsibility? Truth be told, at that point in my life, I really didn't feel like the Lord was telling me it was time to resign. That was the Jesus part of my problem. Jennifer, of course, is my beautiful wife. She had put up with my interest in the LDS faith for many years. I dragged her and the family all over the country, visiting LDS historical sites, and she never complained. She enjoyed our visits up to Nauvoo, but she did not want me to resign from the pastorate, and she *certainly* didn't want me becoming a Latter-day Saint. The third stumbling block to my conversion was a job. Even though I had also worked in a secular occupation most of the years I was pastoring the Church, the salary I made as a pastor made up a significant portion of our income. Were I to convert, I would need a better job to provide for my family, something that could make up the income I would be losing if I quite pastoring. So, until those things could be resolved—Jesus, Jennifer, and a job—I was stuck. I kept feeling this "pull" toward the LDS faith, and yet there were these three barriers blocking my way. This dilemma lasted for four years.

After a bit of a hiatus, in the spring of 2015, I began meeting with the elders (and Brother Ennis) again, and they again challenged me to set a baptismal date. I was more reluctant to do so this time, since I had already had two baptismal dates come and go without me keeping my commitment to be baptized. But they were persistent, and I was curious to see if the Lord's position on my conversion had changed. So, I reluctantly set a date. I selected July 11, 2015, because it was my father's birthday. He had died in an accident eight years prior and, thus, it seemed like a fitting date on which to get baptized. In order to move forward on July 11, I would

> **I DRAGGED HER AND THE FAMILY ALL OVER THE COUNTRY, VISITING LDS HISTORICAL SITES.**

need to resign from the pastorate by June 11. How was I going to do that? How was I going to tell my congregation that I was going to leave them and join the Latter-day Saints?

During my study of the LDS faith, I had occasionally corresponded with various LDS leaders and also with professors at Brigham Young University. I developed a long running dialogue with one professor in particular, Dr. Shon Hopkin. As I was pondering how I was going to say goodbye to my congregation, a thought dawned on me—have Shon write a letter to my church, explaining to them how he felt I could be an effective minister in the LDS community. As crazy as this sounds, I approached Shon with the idea, and he graciously agreed.

The night before I needed to resign my pastorate (in order to meet my July 11 baptismal date), I sat down and talked to my wife about what I was about to do. She was adamantly opposed to the idea. Of course, I was frustrated. That night I prayed, asking the Lord what the purpose was of going through all this, including giving me the impression to have Shon write the letter, if nothing was to come of all of these impressions and promptings. What was I supposed to do? And then the answer came to me very clearly, "Read Shon's letter to the church tomorrow." Even though I had felt inspired by the Spirit to ask Shon to write the letter, as the time approached to read it, I had determined that I wasn't comfortable doing so. Indeed, I told the Lord I didn't *want* to read the letter. I felt like it would just create confusion and would potentially raise more questions than answers.

The next morning, before services began, I was again praying, and again it came to me, "Read Shon's letter." Yet again, in my heart and head, I cried out, "*No*, Lord. I don't think it would be a good idea." The time for the worship service had arrived, and so the time for contemplation was over. I had to act—though what I would do was still up in the air. I gave my sermon, and then we began what Evangelical Churches traditionally call "the invitation." This consists of time set aside at the end of the service, when the congregation sings a hymn and people can come up to the front of the church to pray or counsel with the pastor. During the invitation, I noticed my eighteen-year-old son, B.J., get up out of his seat to make his way to the front of the church. (I should point

> "NO, LORD. I DON'T THINK IT WOULD BE A **GOOD IDEA.**"

out that B.J. shares my interest in LDS history and doctrine, and he had attended every missionary lesson with me.) He knew what had been going on with the missionaries, but he did not know about my conversation with the Lord about Shon's letter. So, what happened next really floored me. B.J. came up to me and said, "Dad, the Holy Spirit just told me that I had to come up here and tell you that you need to read Shon's letter!" B.J. later told me that the prompting was so strong that he felt like, if he didn't come forward, he would have been physically ill. So . . . at the end of the service, though I didn't resign, I read Shon's letter. As I expected, this raised a lot of questions among my congregation. However, in the end, it went a long way in laying a foundation for what would happen four months later.

As the October 2015 general conference approached, I felt prompted to pray and fast about resigning and setting yet *another* baptismal date. This time it wasn't the missionaries pushing; it was me. I remember listening to general conference and yearning to get some clear direction. Several talks ministered directly to me, but one in particular helped clarify the "No" I had received in answer to my prayer four years earlier. The talk I refer to was by Elder Von G. Keetch, of the Seventy. In his talk, Elder Keetch spoke of a barrier in an Australian bay that frustrated surfers because it limited the size of the waves they could catch when surfing. The thing that struck me was what one of the men in the story told the surfers: "Don't be too critical of the barrier," he said. "It's the only thing that's keeping you from being devoured."[2] It was then that it dawned on me why the Lord had said "No" to me four years earlier. There were things out there that I could not see. I had kept feeling this inexplicable pull toward the LDS faith, and so I felt frustrated that God wasn't letting me join. However, there were these clear barriers that kept me from moving forward. I felt that I was stuck. But, as Elder Keetch spoke, I suddenly realized why I was being told "No." The barriers were there to protect me from things that I couldn't see—things that were not as they needed to be in order for my conversion to take place. I don't know what lurked in the proverbial waters. But I realized at that moment that, like the ocean barrier that

> # THE **BARRIERS** WERE THERE TO **PROTECT** ME FROM **THINGS** THAT I COULDN'T SEE.

would be removed when the sharks were gone, when it was right and safe for me to move forward with my conversion, God would remove the barriers that kept me out of the Church. Certain things simply needed to be in place in order to make my conversion possible (for example, a job, a prepared congregation, and my wife's sense of acceptance of my decision). It finally made sense to me, and I told the Lord that I trusted Him, and would wait on him. In the meantime, I would continue to study and meet with the elders when possible. It was as if God was waiting for me to learn that lesson because, as soon as I did, something big happened.

The following Sunday, I was preaching a sermon about the Tower of Babel (Genesis 11). After the flood (in Noah's day), God told the people to scatter. But they *didn't* scatter as He had commanded them. Instead, they built a tower. So, God scattered them by confusing their languages. As I was preaching, a voice exploded in my head, "I TOLD YOU TO GO; NOW GO!" It reverberated in my brain even though I was still preaching my sermon. I could hear words coming out of my mouth, but I have no idea what I was saying. At first my response was, "When did you tell me to go?" But it was clear to me that the promptings I'd received to keep pressing forward were Him telling me to resign the pastorate and begin ministering among the LDS people.

So there it was—my clear answer to move forward. But one problem still remained: how was I going to tell my wife? The last time we talked about this, she was still very much against the idea of my resigning the pastorate. More fasting and praying seemed the only answer to my continuing dilemma! The next Saturday I determined to talk to my wife. We were driving in the car as I explained to her what had happened to me the previous Sunday. I told her that I felt God wanted me to resign as pastor. She laughed and said, "I could have saved you the fasting if you would have told me this sooner. God told me two weeks ago

> I COULD **HEAR WORDS COMING OUT** OF MY MOUTH, BUT I HAVE **NO IDEA** WHAT I WAS **SAYING.**

> "I COULD HAVE **SAVED YOU THE FASTING** IF YOU WOULD HAVE **TOLD ME THIS SOONER.**"

that you were going to resign and He assured me that it would be okay." To say I was surprised would be an understatement! God had actually told her a week before He had told me. She said she was cleaning in the kitchen when this voice just came to her, saying that I was going to resign but that everything would be fine.

With that obstacle removed, my next challenge would be the enormous chore of figuring out how to actually tell my congregation. I loved these people. I wanted them to understand why I was doing this—and to not in any way be hurt by my decision. I wanted all of the key leadership to be in attendance when I made the announcement, so I needed a number of things to

> MY **NEXT CHALLENGE** WOULD BE THE **ENORMOUS CHORE** OF FIGURING OUT HOW TO ACTUALLY **TELL MY CONGREGATION.**

happen so that everyone *could* be in the worship service to hear it from me directly. I didn't want folks hearing this through the grapevine. And yet it seemed impossible for all of these things to fall into place. But, because God is a God of miracles, on the next Sunday everything *did* fall into place. Each of the things I needed to happen in order for me to resign in the best way possible happened. I told the members of my congregation about what had happened—and how God had led me to this point, including explaining to them that Jennifer had received her miraculous confirmation as well. I told them we would stay through the end of the year, but that Sunday, December 28, would be my last Sunday as pastor.

As evidence that God was in the details, within two months I received a promotion at my secular job, and then a cost of living increase, and then a year-end bonus. It didn't come close to making up the income I would be losing come January 1, but it was enough for us to make ends meet, and it was a great reminder that God was in control.

Sunday, January 4, 2016, found me attending testimony meeting at the local LDS ward. I gave my testimony and talked about God's faithfulness. At this point, my wife and I were in agreement that God wanted me to minister among the LDS people, but she didn't want me to become a member. So, in an effort to respect her wishes, I just attended and participated as I could. I also thought it would be nice to visit some other churches. I had been preaching for fifteen years, and that had limited my opportunities to visit other faith traditions. I was looking forward to visiting other churches on occasion, and hearing other preachers. Yet, God only let me visit one other church. During the service the Spirit whispered to me, "This isn't where you are supposed to be." And that was that!

Over the next few months, my wife and I had many conversations about whether or not I should be baptized. She didn't mind if I went to the LDS Church, but she still didn't want me to join. Finally, she told me that if I could tell her that I was "positive" that God wanted me to join, she wouldn't stand in my way. But I wasn't positive. All I knew was that I kept feeling the "pull." But I couldn't say I was "positive" that God wanted me to join the LDS Church—or any church, for that matter. And so the stalemate continued.

Sometime in May 2016, I received an email from Shon Hopkin from BYU. He mentioned that he had just signed up for a conference on medieval literature being hosted by St. Louis University. He wanted to know if we could meet up, since St. Louis was close to where I lived. I readily agreed. I started thinking, *Wouldn't it be great if I could be baptized while Shon was in town? Better yet, what if he was able to perform the baptism?* After all, my correspondence with Shon had played a major role in opening a way for me to even consider baptism.

It is worth noting that there are some significant distinctions between historic Christian theology and LDS theology. As much as I wanted to join the LDS faith, I knew my years as a Baptist would make letting go of some long-held beliefs difficult. I worried that I would be a theological misfit among the Mormons. Shon helped me to see

I WORRIED THAT I WOULD BE A THEOLOGICAL MISFIT AMONG THE MORMONS.

that there was a place for someone with my theological background at the LDS table. I knew that Joseph Smith was a prophet and that the Book of Mormon was the word of God. The other things would take care of themselves. It wasn't an easy process, and it took a lot of dialogue back and forth, but I had reached a point where I thought I could see an opening. My dialogues with Shon had made that possible, and so I wanted him to be the one to perform my baptism. I told the missionaries and Brother Ennis that I was getting baptized, but I told them not to tell anyone else, because I didn't want anyone to get their hopes up in case it fell through like the other three times I had committed to be baptized.

Tuesday, June 14, I was meeting with the elders and Brother Ennis. They asked me how things were progressing and if my wife had given her consent for me to be baptized yet. I asked if it was possible to go ahead and have the baptismal interview but they said they really wanted my wife's consent before they did that.

Something must have happened, because two days later I received a phone call from the zone leader, asking if he could go ahead and conduct the baptismal interview, since he was in the area. So we met at the chapel that Thursday and had the interview.

As June 22 drew closer, I knew something had to happen. Either my wife would give her consent, or the baptismal date would fall through again. I decided to write her a note. I explained what I had been thinking and feeling. I wrote that I still wasn't "positive" that this is what God wanted me to do, but I asked if she would pray about it and seek a confirmation. I gave no deadline, and I didn't say anything about the baptismal date I had set. I left it on her dresser on my way to work. A couple of days passed and she said nothing about the note. Those were difficult days. I felt like a yo-yo, up and down. It was emotionally intense for me. I kept arguing with myself, back and forth. I had a million reasons not to join the LDS Church. But this "pull" wouldn't leave me alone. It kept coming back. Finally, on Monday morning—out of sheer frustration—I said to the Lord, "The heck with it, I'm going for it. If you don't want me to be baptized, please stop me. If you want me to be baptized then make a way, because I

"IF YOU **DON'T WANT** ME TO BE **BAPTIZED**, PLEASE **STOP ME.**"

can't fight this anymore. One way or another, this struggle has to end."

I was two days from my baptismal date, and my wife still had not said a thing to me about the note I had left her. Monday night I had a powerful prompting that I should pray about the note. It just kept hitting me over and over again—pray for that note! Pray for your wife! I knew that I was going to get my answer that night and that whatever answer I received would be *the* answer. I prayed all the way home that night. When I arrived home, sure enough, the note was lying there on my dresser. I didn't want to read it then. So I waited until the next morning. I picked it up off of my dresser and took it with me as I headed to work. When I got into my vehicle, I opened the note. Jennifer had written these words: "If you believe that this is what God wants you to do then I won't stop you." Because of the overwhelming prompting I had to pray for the note the night before, I knew that this was God's answer. When I arrived at work, I texted the missionaries, "Houston, we are 'go' for launch." Wednesday night I was

I KNEW THAT THIS WAS GOD'S ANSWER.

baptized by Brother Hopkin. The following Sunday I was confirmed as a member of The Church of Jesus Christ of Latter-day Saints by Brother Ennis.

In Proverbs 3:5–6 we read, "Trust in the Lord with all thine heart; and lean not unto thine own understanding. In all thy ways acknowledge him, and he shall direct thy paths." I placed my faith and trust in Jesus Christ when I was fourteen years old, and He has directed my path ever since. That path has led me to The Church of Jesus Christ of Latter-day Saints, and I believe that is exactly where He wants me to be. For those readers who may be skeptical of my story, I certainly understand. In the words of the prophet Joseph Smith, "I don't blame any one for not believing my history. If I had not experienced what I have, I would not have believed it myself."[3]

BRYAN

A LESSON TO BE LEARNED

Agency is *absolutely* an eternal principle; and God will *never* rob us of it. It is one of His greatest gifts to humankind. If we choose to do evil, God will allow us to so act. And, if we choose a life of holiness, God will bless us accordingly. But He will *never* force us to act in a way we do not wish to, even when our salvation is at stake. As the hymn goes, "God will force no man to heav'n."[4]

That being said, Bryan's story reminds me of the Book of Jonah; for just as Jonah seemed to have no interest in going to Nineveh and ran from where the Spirit was directing him, so also, Bryan seemed to have plans for his life that ran contrary to God's plan for him. And so that "spiritual pull" kept tugging at the arm of Bryan's soul until he eventually embraced the path God destined him to travel.

Bryan's story is a powerful reminder that although God will always honor our agency, if He needs us for something, He'll keep knocking until we answer Him. And what a blessing that is!

ALONZO

NOTES

1. Ed Decker and Dave Hunt, *The God Makers: A Shocking Exposé of What the Mormon Church Really Believes* (Eugene, Oregon: Harvest House Publishers, 1997).
2. Von G. Keetch, "Blessed and Happy Are Those Who Keep the Commandments of God," *Ensign*, November 2015.
3. *History of the Church*, 6:304–5, 312.
4. "Know This, That Every Soul Is Free," *Hymns*, no. 240.

BUDDHIST

KANOKPHOL "YOUNG" LIMPANASRIPHONG

If you were to ask me whether it is possible for a person to truly change, I would answer your question by telling you my own story of conversion and change.

I was born in Thailand and grew up in Mainland China. I am, by nature, a super happy person. As is common in much of Asia, I don't come from a large family; there are only my parents, my one younger brother, and me. I was raised Buddhist—and faithfully practiced that religion until the time of my conversion. My whole family is Buddhist. In my youth, my parents often had monks living in our home. And one of my favorite things to do was to visit the various temples to discuss Buddhism with the monks who served there. My parents have strong relationships with many of the top monks in Thailand, and my mother has even served as the lead in raising funds to build a large Buddhist temple in Bannock.

My parents are wonderful people who raised me in love and who taught me good manners and appropriate behavior. Being kind to others was a big part of what my parents taught me—and what Buddhism expects of its practitioners. Growing up in their home, each day my parents would encourage me to study the Buddhist scriptures. At the young age of six, I prayed daily, and I sat in the worship room of our small home each night as I read from the Buddhist canon. Regular meditation was a Buddhist practice that greatly blessed my life.

When I think about the important events in my life, one day in particular sticks out in my mind. I was young, and I was about to say my nightly prayer, as I typically did each night before retiring to bed. Suddenly, a thought occurred to me: *why do I have to recite the same prayer every time? Why don't I say whatever is deep down in my heart?* So that night I tried something different. In my heart I offered the Higher Being my thanks and gratitude, and I asked for blessings to be granted to my family. As I prayed, I felt peaceful—and that sense of peace stuck with me.

Years went by, and I continued to be a good Buddhist. I was very blessed by this religion and was happy and content in my faith. So active were my family that we traveled extensively to worship in different Buddhist temples. I had written articles that were published in a Buddhist magazine in China, and I had visited hundreds of temples by the age of fourteen. I enjoyed learning from some of the most respected Buddhist monks in China, Thailand, and Taiwan. At one point, I even thought about becoming a monk so that I could live a life in service to others. But it turned out that this was not God's plan for me.

THERE ARE ONLY **TWO THINGS** IN THIS SO-CALLED "WU TA" (UTAH): **MOUNTAINS AND MORMONS.**

When I was about sixteen years old, I had the opportunity to join an exchange student organization called "Face the World." This is a program that assigns students from all over the world to live with American families for a year, so that the student and the host family can have an international experience. As part of the process, the student who will be coming to the United States gets to pick which state they would like to live in. Excitedly, I narrowed my choices down to California, New York, and Texas. A couple of weeks later I was sad to learn that I would not be going to any of the states I had selected, as I had been assigned to Utah instead. I quickly grabbed my laptop to learn a bit about Utah, and found out that there are only two things in this so-called "Wu Ta" (Utah): mountains and Mormons. I was pretty certain that I was doomed to have an awful experience. Still, for some reason I decided to go anyway. Looking back, I am certain that this was a divine prompting!

My host family in Utah was the Jensons, who lived in a small town called Springville. I soon came to realize that they were wonderful people. I was the same age as one of their daughters, Elizabeth, and the father happened to have served as a missionary in Thailand when he was twenty years old. At the end of the day, the mother oftentimes chatted with me about their religion, mentioning the love she felt for her family, and sharing with me her beliefs about Jesus. As a Buddhist, Jesus was a stranger to me. Yet, as she spoke of Him, I found joy in listening to His story. Living with the Jensons, I started to forget about how remote this place was. Before long, I actually began to find Utah—and its unique people and culture—quite interesting.

Even though Springville was a small town, the kids I met were unique. They were kind and innocent. They didn't drink, smoke, or even swear. I didn't do any of those things either, but, compared to China or Thailand, these people were very different! Because I felt so welcomed, I made many friends during my time in an American high school.

I recognize now how a few specific friends had a life-changing influence on me. Michael was one of those friends. We got to know each other quickly, and one day he asked me about my religion—and whether I believed in God. He also asked me if I would be interested to learn more about the Mormon Church. I said that I would—as I *was* genuinely curious. So, Michael set the terms: "Young, you teach us about Buddha and we will teach you about Jesus."

From that day onward, Mike and I hung out together a lot. It was during my regular visits to his house that I became acquainted with two Mormon missionaries. They taught me about Joseph Smith, the Book of Mormon, and the plan of salvation. When the missionaries invited me to pray, they indicated that I could pray to and communicate with God in my own words. They taught me that God is my Father in Heaven and that families can be together forever. All of these ideas were completely foreign to my upbringing—but I liked them. They felt right to me. One night I finally knelt down and

"YOUNG, YOU TEACH US ABOUT **BUDDHA** AND WE WILL TEACH YOU ABOUT **JESUS**."

45

prayed to God. I felt the same thing I had felt when I was six years old: that peaceful feeling. I started reading the Book of Mormon more carefully and, the more I read it, the more I found myself thinking of one person—Jesus Christ.

During my time in Utah, I was blessed with great friends who never pushed me to join their Church, nor did they force me to do the things that they did. In addition, the friends—Mike, Ben, Connor, Scott, Jared, Austin, Brandon, and many others—were always kind to me, and often shared their testimony of the Church with me. Even though I still considered myself a believing Buddhist, they supported me.

During this time, I regularly met with the missionaries. Though I did so comfortably, in my mind I kept thinking that I really couldn't deny Buddhism or the blessing it had been in my life. So when the elders invited me to be baptized, I quickly said, "No." I felt pretty certain that I would never get baptized in the LDS Church.

My year in the States flew by, and it was about time for me to go back to Thailand. As my departure date approached, I realized how much I had fallen in love with Springville, Utah. Initially, I hadn't wanted to go. Now I hated the thought of leaving. I loved the kindness that people showed me, I loved the culture, and I loved the mountains. Wishing I didn't have to leave, I asked Mike if he thought there was any way that I could somehow come back and live with his family until I had graduated from high school. He talked to his parents, and they both happily agreed to let me live with them. Even now, Mike's family and the Jenson family are like family to me. I am so grateful to these good, generous, and kind people who so richly blessed my life.

The night before I flew back to Thailand for the summer, my friend Connor dropped me off at my host-family's house. But, before I got out from the truck, he told me in a very serious voice that he had something for me. (Connor was usually really funny, and he joked a lot, so I was a bit surprised to see him acting so serious.) He handed me a copy of the Book of Mormon and told me that, because of that book, he knew the Church was true. He then invited me to pray about it *one more time*. I accepted the book and his invitation, and later that night I again knelt down and asked God about the Book of Mormon—I wanted to know if it was truly from Him. It was that same night that I knew the Book of Mormon was actually another testament of Jesus Christ! God had answered my prayer.

Of course, one would assume that—since I knew the Book of Mormon was true—I would immediately want to get baptized. But I was a Buddhist. And Buddhists will sometimes embrace things in other religions without feeling that those things challenge their own Buddhist beliefs or without joining the faith associated with the non-Buddhist thing they have adopted. So, for me, I now knew the Book of Mormon was true, and that convinced me that Jesus was a divine being, that He was one of the gods. I felt my prayer had given me a new piece of knowledge. But that new knowledge didn't cause me to feel I needed to reject Buddhism or become a Mormon. Remaining Buddhist and believing that Jesus was a god posed no contradictions in my mind.

Although I was sad to leave Utah and the United States, I couldn't believe how excited I was to see my parents! It had been nearly a year since we had been together as a family. As I arrived home in Thailand, I realized that, because of the LDS Church, I loved my family a lot more than I used to. Even more surprisingly, I loved telling them about how great the Church was. When I got back to

I NOW KNEW **THE BOOK OF MORMON WAS TRUE,** AND THAT CONVINCED ME THAT **JESUS** WAS A DIVINE BEING, THAT HE **WAS ONE OF THE GODS.**

Thailand, I found that I missed the Church and the Mormon people so much that I located a ward and began attending church there each week. In addition, I prayed diligently to have more of the great feelings I had felt when I was living in Utah.

Before I knew it, my senior year of high school started and I was back in the States. Living with Mike's family, I resumed my regular meetings with the elders. I prayed, read the Book of Mormon and the Bible, went to church weekly, and even enrolled in an early-morning seminary class. I loved the Church more and more every day, but I never forgot that I was a Buddhist. What I was learning colored my Buddhism—but would not replace it. The elders tried everything they could think of to get me to commit to be baptized, but every time they extended the invitation, I said, "No."

One important turning point in my story took place when I attended general conference with Mike's family. This wasn't the first time I had listened to conference, though my recollection of my first experience with it was one of boredom. I remember it being a lot of smart old people talking about stuff that didn't really mean that much to me. But it was a different experience for me to actually sit in the Conference Center and listen to the leaders of the Church speak. I noticed the clock was almost pointing to the six when a man walked in. Suddenly this room with tens of thousands of men in it fell silent as they stood on their feet. Mike's dad leaned over to me and whispered, "That's the prophet, President Thomas S. Monson." A very strong feeling overwhelmed my body as I watched this man walk in and as I heard those words. Even as I write this, I still feel something very special!

The weeks and months continued to pass, and my happy Mormon friends and I graduated from high school. Most of them went on missions, and I stayed in Utah, where I attended a local university. At the time, I was rooming with some young men who had served full-time missions. Now no longer living with Mike's family, I stopped meeting with the missionaries. I figured I'd been taught pretty much everything about the Church, so there didn't seem to be much purpose in investigating it any further. I was content with the thought of being a Buddhist the rest of my life. What's funny, however, is that I kept going to weekly church meetings with the Mormons, and I still read the Book of Mormon multiple times a week. I remember thinking to myself, *Maybe this whole Mormon thing has become a habit.* I just really loved the feeling I got every time I did the things Mormons do.

"MAYBE THIS WHOLE MORMON THING HAS BECOME A HABIT."

One day, my college friends and I were at a concert when we heard someone saying something derogatory about Jesus Christ. All of a sudden I felt very offended. It felt like he was talking badly about my dear friend. This experience caused me to realize that Jesus Christ was more than just a religious figure to me; I felt I could relate myself to Him. I had developed a deep faith in Him.

Not long after that experience, I came home from school one day feeling very excited. This unique feeling inside my soul made me want to do something meaningful, but I didn't know what it meant or what to do. I couldn't sit still, so I started walking aimlessly around the room. When my roommate Ben came home, I explained to him what I was feeling. He smiled and told me that if he were feeling that way, he would go outside and find a place to pray. That sounded right to me, so I decided to do it. As I left the apartment I told my roommates that, if I didn't get back within two hours, they should call the cops and tell them that an Asian was lost in the wilderness.

I was living by the Provo temple at the time, and so I decided to walk toward Provo Canyon, pondering about everything I had learned over the past three years during which I had investigated the LDS Church. As I walked, every testimony that I had heard from my friends and from the missionaries seemed to flood my mind, every scripture that had inspired me to be better filled my heart, and it seemed as though the angels in heaven were singing every hymn that I loved.

I TOLD MY ROOMMATES THAT, IF I DIDN'T GET BACK WITHIN TWO HOURS, THEY SHOULD CALL THE COPS AND TELL THEM THAT AN ASIAN WAS LOST IN THE WILDERNESS.

As I walked, I came to a point where I could see the temple clearly. I looked around, and realizing that no one was there but me, I knelt down and began to pray. I pled, "Father, what should I do?" As I was pondering what to say to Him next, the wind started to blow very loudly. It wasn't just loud, it was also angry, distracting, and overwhelming. I started to feel scared and wondered if praying was the right thing to do. When I was about to give up, the story of the Prophet Joseph Smith came to my mind, and I knew that I couldn't give up, that I must continue my prayer.

I kept calling upon God and, finally, something miraculous happened: every peaceful, uplifting feeling that I could possibly think of came to me as a sort of composite. All of my most spiritual experiences seemed to be combined into one: the prayer that I said when I was six, the first time I prayed to God alone (after the invitation of missionaries), the first time I received an answer that the Book of Mormon was true, the first time I watched the movie *Joseph Smith: Prophet of the Restoration* at Temple Square, the first time that I saw President Monson in real life, the first time I found out that I loved Jesus Christ. *All of the attending feelings of each of those experiences hit my soul so hard!* And then I heard these words: "My son, don't deny Me and My Only Begotten Son. You know all you have learned is true. Go and do the things that you know you need to do."

I was absolutely overwhelmed by the experience, but I knew exactly what God wanted me to do. I got up, and with my eyes full of tears, I gazed at the beautiful temple. Without even thinking about what I was doing, my hand reached into my pocket, and before I knew it, I was on the phone with Mike's dad. I wanted to explain to him what I was feeling, but I was not able to speak. Nothing came out of my mouth except heavy breathing. He asked me if I was all right, and all I could say was, "Dad, I'm ready to be baptized."

"DAD, I'M **READY** TO BE **BAPTIZED**."

That night, as I knelt down again to pray, I thanked God for His answer that day, and also for all of the answers He had granted me over the last few years. I apologized for my ignorance and pride, and I promised Him that for the rest of my life I would share His love with all of His children—including through serving a full-time mission.

October 9, 2010, is a day I will always remember. It's the day that Mike and I, dressed in white, entered the baptismal font, and he baptized me a member of The Church of Jesus Christ of Latter-day Saints. Hundreds of people who had helped me, and who had been an example to me along the way, stood as witnesses to God's ability to change the life of a prideful man. As I entered the waters of baptism, I saw the beautiful faces of my loved ones and felt the heavens open and the angels singing. After I was baptized, I was able to share my testimony with the people who loved me and whom I loved!

I am so very grateful to all who were there that day, and to those who helped me to find the true Church of Jesus Christ. Even more so, I am grateful that God and His Son were there by my side throughout my journey. I witnessed something very special the day of my baptism, and by personal experience—and with a sure conviction—I know God the Father and Christ, His Son, truly live! They have living, glorified bodies! I cannot deny it!

My parents were remarkably supportive of me when I told them that I had decided to join the Church. While we have always been an incredibly close family, my parents also allowed me (from a very young age) to be an independent person who made my own decisions. So they trusted me to think things through—and to make wise and reasoned life decisions. Throughout my conversion process, I spoke regularly to my parents, and let them know what was happening every step of the way. Thus, they were not surprised when I told them I was going to be baptized. My mother's counsel to me was simply, "Be the best member of

"BE THE **BEST MEMBER** OF THE CHURCH THAT YOU CAN."

the Church that you can." The day after I told them that I was going to join, my father sent me an email quoting Doctrine and Covenants section four. (He had spent time studying about the Church, and had found this particular passage of LDS scripture especially poignant in light of my decision to be baptized.) To this day, my parents often feed the LDS missionaries when they see them.

I bear my witness that The Church of Jesus Christ of Latter-day Saints is the true Church of Christ! God hears and answers our prayers. I know that Jesus Christ wrought the Atonement on our behalf. He is our Savior! He is resurrected, and we shall all see Him in the flesh one day! In 1820, Joseph Smith saw God the Father and His Son Jesus Christ in the flesh and, after that event, the Church was restored. The Book of Mormon and the Holy Bible are the words of God. We also have a modern-day living prophet who can lead us and guide us so that we can live meaningful, happy, and productive lives. God's purpose is to help us become like Him and to bind family members together through time and eternity. I know all these things are true, because I asked God, and He cared! I love Him, so I will serve Him throughout my life.

YOUNG

A LESSON TO BE LEARNED

To the Nephites, Jesus said, "What manner of men ought ye to be? Verily I say unto you, even as I am" (3 Nephi 27:27). And Alma recorded that the bad example of members of the Church caused nonmembers to reject the gospel, and even to sin. (See Alma 4:11 and 39:11.) In the story of Young's conversion, we see the importance that example plays in drawing others to the Church and to Christ. Young testified of the influence his friends had on his desire to know if the Church was true. Even his Buddhist mother understood this principle, when she counseled her son, "Be the best member of the Church that you can." If Latter-day Saints wish to see the gospel grow at a faster rate than it currently is, they should realize that the answer isn't more eighteen- and nineteen-year-old missionaries. The answer is more members who live lives of love, kindness, faith, and friendliness. *That* is what will cause an increase in conversions!

ALONZO

EPISCOPALIAN AND LUTHERAN

MEREDITH AND RANDALL CASTO

Ours is a most improbable story. It is a story of two professional clergy from the Episcopal and Lutheran faith traditions who experienced the unexpected (and arguably inconvenient) movement of the Holy Spirit. It was a movement that would both humble and enliven us. It was a movement that would lead us in the discovery of answers to theological questions previously unanswered. The movement of the Spirit would satisfy us beyond measure—and challenge us anew each day!

We do not consider our experiences to be "conversion" stories. We do not consider ourselves to be "converts"; we did not "convert" from anything. Instead, we considered our experiences as ones of enlightened faith.

We were already believers in the atoning power of Jesus Christ. We already subscribed to the transformative work of the Holy Spirit to open our hearts to both our sinfulness and our forgiveness.

> WE DO NOT CONSIDER OURSELVES TO BE "**CONVERTS**"; WE DID NOT "CONVERT" FROM ANYTHING.

We already knew that God loved us beyond measure. What we did *not* know, however, would make such a difference for us in understanding the "fullness" of the gospel.

What we learned was that priesthood authority (and heavenly power) was once again restored to the earth and that it had been taken from the earth upon the death of the Apostles. We discovered that spouses and families could be together forever, sealed by the authority of the restored priesthood. We learned that the atoning power of Christ's sacrifice could not only fill us with the knowledge of forgiveness but also then create in us a powerful new awareness of eternity—and our God-designed part in it. We learned all of this and so much more.

We came to understand what the Church means when it refers to "the fullness of the gospel"—the "fullness" restored to the earth through the work and witness of the prophet Joseph Smith—and how our Lord directed the angel Moroni and others to be vehicles through which an additional testimony of Jesus Christ would be gifted to the world through the Book of Mormon. We had it confirmed in our hearts that the Mormons are not a "cult" (as some profess), but rather a body of believers in Christ who embrace the "fullness of the gospel" and who are called to share it with the world.

But enough of this preamble. It is on now to our individual (and intertwined) stories of enlightened faith. We pray that our story may be a source of encouragement for you—that you may see our story as every-one's story, or so the Lord intends. For He seeks the movement of the Spirit, leading to eternal life, through Jesus Christ—the Life of the Word.

MEREDITH

I was hungry.

Not the hunger that can be satisfied with a meal. But that deep, abiding hunger I could never seem to quell. It was a hunger that was palpable. It was a hunger that brought with it a great depth of sadness, loneliness, and longing for something more. When Jesus commanded Peter to "feed my sheep" (see John 21), He was speaking not only of literally feeding those who were hungry. The Only Begotten Son was instructing Peter to feed the hungry with the only thing that could truly quell their hunger: the good news of Christ's Atonement. But not that *only*. As I discovered, there's more to the story that I didn't know, and that's why *I* was *so* hungry.

I had been a regular churchgoer my entire life, even attending on my own in high school. During the fall semester of my sophomore year of college, I felt God calling me to the ordained ministry. Thus, following college, I attended seminary, completed my master's degree in Divinity, and was ordained into the priesthood in the Episcopal Church. In 2007, at the age of twenty-six, I became the head pastor of two rural churches. Following two years serving those churches, I began to work as a chaplain at a retirement community of four hundred to five hundred residents. It was a vibrant ministry! I loved so much about it!

And yet, I was still hungry.

Shortly thereafter I experienced an exceedingly painful end to my marriage—an end that came because of abuse inflicted upon me by the man who was then my spouse. The divorce was made even more painful when the church I had attended and served in my whole life was unable to offer the support I so needed. Remarkably, in the midst of that pain, I sensed there was something more. I just didn't know where to find it. I knew that I was a lost sheep and had been my whole life. I sensed home was somewhere, but could not seem to locate it. I kept waiting for the Lord to leave the ninety and nine and come find me—the one lost sheep.

And yet, I was so accustomed to hunger that I didn't know any different. So I remained hungry.

I KEPT WAITING FOR THE LORD TO **LEAVE THE NINETY AND NINE** AND COME FIND ME—**THE ONE LOST SHEEP.**

By the grace of God, I found love and companionship—honor, respect, protection, and peace—in Randy. This incredible man would eventually become my husband. But Heavenly Father had something additional in mind for us, as a yet-unmarried couple, to experience. It was something that would strengthen our already strong love and respect for one another. It was something that would quell the hunger.

During the summer and fall of 2012, Randy and I were keen to watch and pay attention to the political campaigns. As a lifetime voter for Democrat candidates and a staunch liberal, it had never occurred to me to pay attention to *those* Republicans my family had raised me to believe were absolutely crazy! With Randy's encouragement, the two of us watched the Republican National Convention (RNC). I felt the Spirit's presence as I heard stories of how Mitt Romney had served in the LDS Church. I felt the Spirit's presence as I listened to Ann Romney talk about love of family and her husband. The way in which she authentically respected him, and he honored her, moved me to tears. I felt a small spark in me come to life.

But, again, I was used to being hungry—I didn't know anything else. So I remained hungry.

Shortly following the RNC, I had the opportunity to hear two LDS women speak at the retirement community I was serving. My mind and heart were relatively closed, because I thought I knew all about the Mormons. In high school, I actually investigated the LDS Church! I only did so because I wanted to date a cute Mormon boy named Victor. His parents had two rules for dating their son: 1) we had to be sixteen (which I now know is a teaching of the Church and not just a rule they made up!), and 2) I had to become a Mormon. So I started investigating. I attended sacrament meeting and Sunday School a few Sundays, wrote a term paper on the Church—even interviewed a bishop! But then my mother put a stop to all of that. "We are liberals. We are Democrats. We are not Mormons!" she would say. And so, my time of investigation ended. I really wanted to date this Mormon boy, but I couldn't convert,

"WE ARE LIBERALS. WE ARE DEMOCRATS. **WE ARE NOT MORMONS!**"

so we couldn't officially date. I was hurt and angry. And I was convinced that I knew everything about the Mormon Church. Despite my experience of listening to the RNC, I had no intention of being taught anything new about the Mormons by these two LDS women. How could anyone teach me if I already knew *everything*?

The two women, members of a local LDS congregation, brought with them "The Family: A Proclamation to the World." Immediately upon receiving it, I began reading. I was struck by a statement toward the end: "We warn that individuals . . . who abuse [his or her] spouse . . . will one day stand accountable before God."[1] The Church was not saying this for my benefit. They were proclaiming this truth to the world and had no shame in doing so. I felt a deep comfort come over me, given my experience with spousal abuse, and began to engage these two women in conversation. In front of approximately twenty of my retirement community congregants, I talked about how much I enjoyed watching the RNC. I explained that as I was watching it, and feeling something really good (which I now know was the Spirit), I said, "I want some of that!" Without missing a beat, one of the LDS women (Amy) said, "Well, you know, Meredith, it's never too late."

I want to take a moment to paint a picture of what this moment entailed. I was wearing my clericals (all black clothing with a white collar—not unlike what one would see a Roman Catholic priest wearing) and was the spiritual leader of a four- to five-hundred-member community, some of whom were present. And yet, the Holy Spirit gave this sister the courage to say what I think few would have had the courage to say. To a pastor in another church she spoke words that will be forever ingrained in my mind. When she said those words, I was stunned. For weeks, they replayed in my head. And now, years later, I'm still talking about those words, sharing them with you.

Amy and I met a few times, taking long walks, and talking about mental health—a passionate topic for both of us. But each time, we eventually ended up talking about the Church. Amy was not pushy. I never felt she was proselyting. We were just walking.

But, I had been hungry my whole life. It was a normal feeling for me, and one that I didn't feel I would ever escape in this life. And so, I stayed hungry.

Amy and her husband, Mark, invited me to go sailing with them. As a lifetime sailor, and racer of sailboats, I could not fathom saying, "No." And so, on a Saturday in October 2012, I went sailing with them. Following our eventful sailing trip, they invited me to stay for lunch. As it turned out, we would just "happen" to be watching a session of general conference while eating. As I sat and ate, I listened. There was a part of me that didn't want to listen. After all, I already knew *everything* about the Mormons. But the Spirit was so strong, I had no choice. That Saturday afternoon in October, I listened to men speak about God, the Holy Spirit, family, and happiness in a way that I had never heard before. Apparently, we're supposed to be happy. No one ever told me that before! I was moved to tears. Amy, Mark and I spoke at length about my experience with my divorce, about the pain, about Heavenly Father, and God's Spirit, and God's plan of salvation. Again, I was moved to tears. What was that feeling?

For the first time in my life, I wasn't hungry. I was filled. And I wanted more of it.

Following my time with Mark and Amy, I went to Randy and told him we needed to investigate the LDS church.

RANDY

My whole life I have had a peculiar natural faith and trust in God, an awareness of God's love, mercy, and loyalty. Ever since I was a young boy, I had a "strange" (or at least to me it was strange) awareness of the Almighty. I just "knew" in my heart that God lived. There was always this "strange sensation" (for lack of a better term) that God knew and loved me. In the midst of my confusions with the world, I "knew" that God was watching over me. Consequently, as a little boy—growing up Roman Catholic—I felt the desire to become a priest. That desire was one not focused on the worship life of the Church, but on the special awareness to be called and set apart for a particular purpose—God's glory.

As I grew, I came to an understanding that our Lord was not calling me to the Catholic priesthood but, rather, to serve in other ways. With marriage and children, I came to understand that serving the Lord was possible in myriad ways. Yet my sense of awareness of the priesthood remained with me until I eventually entered formal theological training (in my forties) to become a priest/pastor in the Lutheran tradition. It was a strong calling. In a way, this satiated my sense of calling to the priesthood; and yet there was still much lacking, still much that I questioned that didn't make sense. The years in formal training and education taught me about scripture and the practices of worship and the mechanics of professional clergy. But still, many questions remained—theological and otherwise. I would go on to serve several large congregations as a senior pastor, preaching and teaching, leading in worship, and supervising pastor interns. Later though, and sadly, for a variety of reasons, my marriage ended in divorce.

MANY QUESTIONS REMAINED— THEOLOGICAL AND OTHERWISE.

This was a deeply traumatic time and, yet, through it all I felt sustained by that "peculiar natural faith and trust in God." Through this process I found myself alone dealing with a crisis of faith in the Church, ultimately falling away and resigning from the Church's active clergy roster. I had struggled with the lack of support I had received from the Lutheran bishop during my divorce. But, even worse, I struggled with the movement of the Church's doctrine and polity to the left—very far to the left. In the end, I would learn that it was not a falling away from my faith that I was experiencing, but rather a new step forward toward something eternally greater to which the Lord was leading me.

Meredith and I had known each other professionally for several years. Unknown to each other, we had both gone through difficult divorces. We both had faced a crisis of faith and were yearning for something more, something true. We both were hungry. We listened to and cared for each other during this time of healing. Over time we discovered that, much to our surprise, we had fallen in love. We would learn that the Lord had much in store for us!

MUCH TO OUR SURPRISE, WE HAD FALLEN IN LOVE.

After boating with Mark and Amy (I referred to them as "the Mormons"), Meredith called me and shared with me the feeling she had while being with them and while watching general conference. She wanted to know if we could have a conversation about it. I was mildly surprised by her comments, but delighted to be in conversation with her. Both of our hearts were always open to things related to the work of the Spirit. She shared that she was deeply moved by the awareness of the Spirit working through the conference speakers and asked that we pray about how the Lord might be leading us. I agreed. I was quite skeptical, but I agreed.

Now, I am by nature and nurture particularly discerning and, thus, I am not easily swayed. I am not a skeptic, but rather one who needs to have a substantial understanding before I can be moved. I am open to being moved, . . . it just takes work! By training and education, I am a theologian who revels in delving into scripture and relishes the Spirit leading me to understand more deeply the workings of our Creator. I love sharing and teaching from the scriptures. Ever since I was a little boy, I have felt that "peculiar natural faith and trust in God." I have always sensed God's faithful love and care—preeminently exemplified in and through Jesus. I was indeed a Christian whose faith and trust was centered in the *all-sufficient work* of Christ, to the glory of the Father. For me, it was the mainline Christian understanding that was the witness of the truth. Well . . .

Meredith and I began to meet regularly with Mark and Amy. In addition, over ensuing months, we met with a raft of young missionaries. We all loved the time we spent together. Everyone was so patient with us— well, really they were patient with *me*. We pressed the envelope on myriad topics, from the sacraments, to grace, to the Trinity, to forgiveness, to the law, to the cross, to the plan of salvation, and even Kolob! The questions were not posed argumentatively but in an effort to seek understanding. Meredith and I read the Book of Mormon. The richness and depth of that book simply sealed the deal for us. We both recognized that Joseph could not have made it up. It was *far* too substantive. Our testimony of everything else flowed from that revelation. Of course, in addition to the Book of Mormon, we read the Doctrine and Covenants and the Pearl of Great Price. We admit that we did not read it all, but we read enough, together, that the Spirit witnessed to our hearts that it was all true. Remarkably, it was true!

Meredith was way ahead of me. I must acknowledge that it was *I* who was far behind in coming to know the truth about Joseph Smith, the Restoration of the gospel, the restoration of the priesthood, and our Lord's witness in these latter days. This was not a continuation of the Reformation but, rather, a *Restoration*. This was a key distinction for me—for us.

Once the Spirit lovingly walked me to the place of convergence— when, theologically and spiritually, it all made sense—it was for me a great revelation. Not entirely unlike, surely, Saul's experience on the road to Damascus (dare I raise the comparison)! My faith had been enlightened with the fullness of the truth,

THE **TRUTH** HAS BEEN HIDDEN IN **PLAIN SIGHT!**

and it then occurred to me: *Everyone needs to know about this. If this is the fullness of the truth*—and it is—*then my brothers and sisters need to know of it. The truth has been hidden in plain sight!*

MEREDITH

We began to attend church. For the first time in my life, I felt safe in church. I felt comfort. I felt moved. I felt my heart sparked back to life as Randy and I—together—attended church and met with Mark and Amy and the missionaries. I felt enlivened as I participated in Relief Society and heard women speak so lovingly about the honor of being women, wives, and mothers—caring for their families as Heavenly Father intended. For the first time in my life, I realized that being a woman was enough. I didn't need to try to fill the roles that men fill. I didn't need to try and be more powerful (according to the world's standards) or more aggressive. I could be a woman, wife, and mother, as God intended. And there was nothing more honorable than that. Finally, I felt free. I no longer needed to try and be someone I wasn't. In Relief Society, I was encouraged to be who Heavenly Father created me to be. I had never felt like such a powerful and strong woman!

During this time of investigation, Randy and I were married. Because of our attending the LDS church, there was an even holier aspect to our marriage. The love, honor, and respect we had for one another was only heightened by being surrounded by people who lived their lives with the same understanding of mutual love, honor, and respect.

The Holy Spirit continued to be at work in our hearts, confirming the truth of His restored gospel. I realized that when Jesus commanded Peter to "feed my sheep," He was not speaking only of the teachings presented in the Bible; Jesus was speaking to us, instructing us to "feed" his sheep with the "fullness" of the gospel—because only in the fullness of the gospel can we find ourselves no longer hungry.

Randy and I began to work toward my being able to leave my job and leave the ordained ministry altogether. On Friday, June 14, 2013, I left work, along with the ordained ministry. I took off my clericals for the last time, changed into church clothes, and Randy and I experienced the great wonder of baptism that evening.

I AM **NOT LONELY** OR LONGING FOR SOMETHING MORE. **I HAVE COME HOME.**

I have never looked back. Why would I? Between my marriage, baptism, and the building up of our family, I am happy. I am not hungry anymore. Even in the midst of the difficulties we face—and there is always adversity in life—I am not hungry. I am not lonely or longing for something more. I have come home.

RANDY

I have come to understand that Heavenly Father's patience with me enabled me to come to a place of understanding; not only an understanding of LDS theology but also of how it is distinct from that of mainline Christianity. This is not one more "reformed" religion, but rather a "revelation of restoration." I began to sense that I was being prepared to proclaim this message to mainline Christianity. There are so many who are hurting, who feel disenfranchised, who feel let down, and who have questions that can never be answered outside the fullness of the gospel. There are so many who yearn for righteousness and yet whose spiritual perception is clouded. This, I suppose, is what it means to be in the spiritual wilderness (the Great Apostasy).

By the grace of God, I know that Joseph Smith was indeed the vehicle through whom our Lord would bring about the Restoration of the gospel, the priesthood authority, and the fullness of the Church as our Lord intended. Is this not the Good News in these latter days?

Jesus has shined a great light, and the darkness of these last days will not overcome it. Indeed, the time of spiritual darkness has ended. Our Lord's proclamation of "release to the captives" is once again restored to the earth to be a blessing for all people.

By the grace of God, I know that Joseph was given the Spirit-led ability to translate the additional revelation of Jesus Christ, made known through the Book of Mormon. My testimony is that John the Baptist and Peter, James, and John restored to the earth the God-given authority of the lesser and greater priesthoods. I truly know that, in these latter-days, there is a hastening to our Lord's work—through the Church—to gather in the House of Israel. Truly the fields are white for the harvest! Just speak with any of the over seventy thousand young missionaries around the world who are taking eighteen months to two years of their lives to share this good news with others!

MEREDITH AND RANDY

It's interesting to think of this experience as a "coming home." It allows us to see this story not as one of conversion, but of return. In their book, *The God Who Weeps: How Mormonism Makes Sense of Life*, Terryl and Fiona Givens write, "In turning to God, . . . we are not converting—but reverting—to a holy model, 'speed[ing] back to the eternal light, children to the Father.'"[2]

Our lives haven't "changed" by joining the LDS Church; our lives have become *alive*! We have finally started living! We are no longer hungry, lonely, or longing. Not because we've changed—but because we've come home. We are happy, because—individually, and as a family—we have come "back to the eternal light, children to the Father." We are home. We aren't hungry. We are joyful in the fullness of the gospel. We are sealed in marriage for

> WE ARE **ONE IN** OUR LORD'S FULLNESS.

time and all eternity. Our children are sealed to us as family for time and eternity. We are one in our Lord's fullness.

We share our stories in the Name of the One who loves us more than our finite minds can even begin to understand; whose yearning is that not one of us would hunger ever again; whose desire is that we all come home.

MEREDITH AND RANDY

A LESSON TO BE LEARNED

Meredith and Randy's conversion stories remind us of the psalmist, who declared of the "hungry and thirsty" and "soul-fainted": "Oh that men would praise the LORD for his goodness, and for his wonderful works to the children of men! For he satisfieth the longing soul, and filleth the hungry soul with goodness" (Psalm 107:5, 8–9).

At times, all of us long for something. Longing can be painful, particularly if it is prolonged. And yet, as Meredith and Randy have shown, longing can be a source of motivation. At times, God gives us a deep and abiding longing because He knows that is the very thing that will cause us to seek to satiate that craving. And, as in the case of Meredith and Randy, it can lead to conversion. In their case, it brought them into the restored gospel. But, in the case of each of us, a longing for something better—a life more holy, happy, or spiritually alive—can lead us to a deeper and more abiding conversion to Christ and the principles He taught. Thus, spiritual longing is a gift from God, if we will seek to satiate it.

ALONZO

NOTES

1. "The Family: A Proclamation to the World," *Ensign*, November 2010, 129.
2. Terryl Givens and Fiona Givens, *The God Who Weeps: How Mormonism Makes Sense of Life* (Ensign Peak, 2012), 40.

EVERYTHING

KEONGUK KIM

I was born in 1978 to Roman Catholic parents in the Province of Jeolla-namdo, which is in the southwest portion of South Korea. My parents were active in their faith and, thus, I attended the Catholic Church regularly from the time I was born. When I was in the fourth grade, my family moved to Seoul, and that changed a number of things in our lives. For one, though we had regularly attended Mass in Jeolla-namdo, once in Seoul, our lives became inordinately busy. We didn't seek out the Church there, and so we really stopped participating in any significant way in organized religion.

As time passed and I grew older, I began to have many questions about life, its purpose, and my place in it and the world. Such questions are natural, I suppose, but they weighed on me, and I found that I thought about them a great deal. However, around the time I began my senior year of high school, I came to the conclusion that I wasn't going to be able to find answers to such questions—so I decided I would just stop worrying about them. Because my Christian

I BEGAN TO HAVE MANY QUESTIONS ABOUT LIFE, ITS PURPOSE, AND MY PLACE IN IT AND THE WORLD.

upbringing and faith didn't seem to hold the answers to my questions, I eventually began to look for peace and direction in the Buddhist tradition. (Buddhism encourages its practitioners to not worry, nor to be distracted by the world and its enticements. After years of unanswered questions, this seemed a good place to turn.) As time went on, I engaged more and more in Buddhist practice. I read their books, and spent a great deal of time contemplating the meaning of life. The more I lived Buddhism, the more I began to think Buddhism might just have the answers to the questions that plagued me as a youth. So I set out to find a Buddhist temple so that I could do whatever people do to "join" the Buddhist faith.

I SET OUT TO **FIND A BUDDHIST TEMPLE** SO THAT I COULD DO WHATEVER PEOPLE DO TO **"JOIN" THE BUDDHIST FAITH.**

However, my parents had not given me permission to join and, when they discovered that I had done so without speaking to them first, they grounded me for several days as a punishment for my lack of filial piety, or lack of respect for them and their wishes. (In many Asian religions, and certainly in Korean culture, one is to show respect and honor to one's parents. One places them and their wishes before one's own desires. I had not done so, and my parents were quite unhappy about that.)

That year I had a teacher who was quite open with his religion. He was Presbyterian. At some point I learned that, and we discussed his religion and my questions a bit. Over time he invited me to attend the Presbyterian Church with him, which I did. I initially felt content there, and so I began to consider myself a Presbyterian.

As I began to attend each week, I can honestly say that I felt a great deal of peace. I enjoyed the people and the teachings and

I BEGAN TO CONSIDER MYSELF A **PRESBYTERIAN.**

rather enjoyed going to their various meetings. Consequently, I continued to attend the Presbyterian Church into my college years.

During my second year at the university, my trajectory shifted somewhat. While I was not discontent in the church I was attending, I met a man on the street one day and, in the midst of our conversation, he informed me that he attended what he called the Good News Mission

Church or Kuwŏnp'a, as it is colloquially known in South Korea. My acquaintance informed me that all a person needed to do in order to receive salvation was to believe in Jesus's sacrifice on his or her behalf. He also indicated that doing "good works" and seeking to keep "commandments" wasn't necessary in order to go to heaven. God didn't care about such things, because faith in Him was what saved a person—not a life of obedience and works. He said that, no matter how evil one's life was, if one had faith in Christ as his or her personal savior, one would go to heaven. He indicated that the opposite was also true: if you lived a righteous and obedient life, but didn't accept Jesus, you would go to hell. Well, I was disturbed by what he said. I just couldn't believe that this was how God would decide who was saved and who was damned. Nevertheless, my new friend invited me to study the Bible with him so that he could show me these truths as they were taught in God's word. I agreed to. However, as we discussed the Bible together, I found that I still did not agree with his interpretation of God's plan for His children; yet I also quickly sensed that I did not have the knowledge of the Bible necessary to show him that he was misinterpreting the passages he was quoting.

I determined that I should go talk to my teacher, who introduced me to the Presbyterian Church, and see what he thought of this teaching. I was sure he would know Bible verses that would prove the Good News Mission Church's doctrines were wrong. (He was serving as a missionary in the Presbyterian Church at that time.) To my surprise, he couldn't disprove their doctrinal claims—nor could the Presbyterian pastor. I was at a loss as to what to do. Were the things the Good News Mission Church was teaching correct? I still didn't feel good about them, but if they were wrong, why couldn't the Presbyterians show that from the Bible? Since I wasn't able to get any help from my pastor nor my missionary friend, I decided that I would have to figure this out on my own. I determined that the best way to do this was to attended the Good News Mission Church and learn their doctrines for myself. Then ideally I would be able to see why I felt so uncomfortable with their teachings.

> WERE THE THINGS **THE GOOD NEWS MISSION CHURCH** WAS TEACHING CORRECT?

This seemed to me a good solution to my dilemma, so I began to attend the services regularly.

I took seriously my commitment to find out if the Good News Mission Church was teaching true doctrine. I listened to the Kuwŏnp'a Pastor Ock Soo Park's recorded sermons for at least three hours every day, and I regularly traveled to the Church's large seminars that were held in Gwangju and Daejeon Korea. Though I was heavily involved for three months, I still didn't feel able to refute their doctrines because of my lack of training in the Bible. Yet, I continued to feel very uneasy about what they were teaching. This left me quite frustrated. So I determined that it was probably best if I set all of this aside and focused instead on other things in my life. My engagement in the Good News Mission Church had not brought me peace. On the contrary, it had brought a fair amount of angst into my life. Therefore, I decided to shift my attention to developing job skills so that I could land secure employment. That seemed a better use of my personal time.

After a fair amount of contemplation of my skills and academic interests, I decided to become a nuclear technician. I began my schooling for this vocation and, after becoming certified, I deferred my third year of university education because of a job opportunity that arose at a company in the neighboring province of Kyeonggi-do, the most populous province in South Korea.

While living in Kyeonggi-do, I started attending the Methodist Church pretty regularly. However, after about two months of doing so, I met one of Jehovah's Witnesses. He offered me a copy of *The Watchtower*, but I told him I already attended church and wasn't really interested in learning about another faith. He replied, in a rather welcoming voice,

WHILE LIVING IN KYEONGGI-DO, I STARTED ATTENDING THE METHODIST CHURCH PRETTY REGULARLY.

"Well then, would you like to have a Bible discussion together? If I'm wrong, you could continue going to your church, but in the event that *you're* wrong, it wouldn't be good to continue going to the Methodist Church, you know. Either way, since—in the eyes of God—there is only one truth, I think it would be a good thing to find out if this is it." What he said struck me as valid. So, I made an appointment with him for two days later.

When we met for our Bible study, he asked if, perchance, there was anything I had been wondering about with regards to the Bible. Surprised, I told him "Yes," I had two questions that had been on my mind. First, over the last two days I had been wondering why it is that Jehovah's Witnesses refuse to serve in the military. (In South Korea, every able-bodied young man must serve a minimum of two years in the military, and refusing to do so is seen by many Koreans as extremely anti-patriotic and very strange.)

He answered my question with a scripture. He said, "According to Isaiah 2:4, in the last days Jehovah's people will go to the mountain of the Lord." According to this Witness brother, the people Isaiah was seeing were those who do not practice war and do not lift swords against other humans. He explained that "this is a better way to live, and it is more peaceful and loving than how much of the world lives today." In addition, he said, "Think of World War II. There were Methodists living in Germany and also in France. If they each participated in the war, and killed each other, could they honestly say that they loved their brothers, as Jesus had commanded them to (see 1 John 4:21)? Jehovah's Witnesses take quite literally the command to love our brothers; we could not join the military and then take the lives of our brothers and sisters—simply because they come from a different country. Thus, we don't serve in the military."

Satisfied with his answer, I asked the second question that had been on my mind since we met two days earlier: Why don't Jehovah's Witnesses accept blood transfusions? He turned to Acts 15:20, in the Bible, and read: "But . . . abstain from things polluted by idols, from sexual immorality, from what is strangled, and from blood" (New World Translation). He went on to say that, "Ever since Old Testament times, blood has symbolized life. The Bible says 'the life of the flesh is in the blood' (NWT Leviticus 17:11). Clearly blood is a divine thing. As the source of life, Jehovah has provided definite instructions regarding its use, and we choose to obey Jehovah's directives."

For the first time in a long time, I felt that I had found answers to my questions through the Bible. I was thrilled! Why could the others not do what this brother had done for me? So happy was I about the way that he had gone to the scriptures to answer my questions, I decided I would become one of Jehovah's Witnesses.

I DECIDED I WOULD BECOME ONE OF **JEHOVAH'S WITNESSES.**

Of course, becoming a Witness is no speedy process. Prior to being baptized, Jehovah's Witnesses require that you study for many months—in some cases, even years— before you get baptized. (They want to ensure that the convert fully believes the teachings of the organization.) So, I began my studies. Every day I read the Bible for *at least* four hours, and most evenings I met with Witnesses (for at least an hour) to discuss their teachings and beliefs. In the process, I learned how to interpret the Bible the Witness way, and I received a lot of guidance from the one-on-one home visits. I began to think like a Witness, and see in the scriptures what the Witnesses saw in the scriptures.

After six months of dedicated study—and establishing that I was an educated believer in the teachings of the Watch Tower Bible and Tract Society, I qualified myself to be baptized. The Elders of the congregation tested my knowledge of the scriptures for two hours a day over a three-day period. After I had proved my knowledge, and attested to the elders that I was living an honest and chaste life, they said it would be good for me to be baptized. Witnesses hold their baptisms at their biannual conferences. The next one would be the coming fall, so I anticipated being baptized then.

After being baptized, I engaged in other aspects of my newfound religion. For example, Witnesses are known for their faithful proselyting. So, I proselyted for at least fifteen hours every month. I did this faithfully for a year and eight months; but had to stop when I reached the age that I was required by the South Korean government to start my required two-years of military service. Because of what the Witnesses had taught me, I didn't want to join the army, and I had already decided to go to prison instead of joining the military. However, when I informed my parents of my decision, they were incredibly unhappy with me and opposed my decision in the most stringent manner. This made me question whether I was making the right decision by not enlisting in the military. Consequently, I began worrying about how committed I was to God. Did I really have faith like Abraham? Abraham completely trusted God—to the degree that he was willing to take the life of his son when asked of God, believing in the resurrection and God's omniscient will. Did I have that kind of faith, that kind of trust in God? I suddenly realized that I did not. Nor did I have an assurance of my salvation. I suddenly felt very frustrated, and my mind began to be flooded with seemingly random religious questions: When Adam and Eve picked the fruit of the Tree of Knowledge of Good and Evil, why did God not stop them? If the Lord is omnipotent, wouldn't it be right for Him to prevent tragedy from striking the innocent? Why do we have to suffer for the mistakes of Adam and Eve? Suddenly the Witnesses' answers to these questions didn't satisfy me. Indeed, none of the churches I had looked into offered satisfying answers to these questions.

Because I now realized that I actually wasn't certain about my beliefs or my salvation, I was resolved that I could not worship with Jehovah's Witnesses any longer. What I had thought I was sure of, I realized I simply was not. I didn't want to just walk away from the people and organization that had been such a large part of my life for the previous two years. Indeed, I felt that I *needed* to

NONE OF THE CHURCHES I HAD LOOKED INTO OFFERED SATISFYING ANSWERS TO THESE QUESTIONS.

explain my reasons for leaving. So, I wrote a letter to the elders over my congregation, explaining—among other things—that I knew that there was only one God and that, because God was just, there could only be one organization that He recognized. However, I felt that I now knew for certain that it was *not* Jehovah's Witnesses. Because saying something like this would be considered by Witnesses a "sin against the Holy Spirit," I knew that it would not be well received. In the end, I decided that it was best that I not deliver the letter. So, I just quietly left the organization.

WHILE ENLISTED, I ATTENDED THE WORSHIP SERVICES FOR THE SHINCHEONJI CHURCH.

After I left Jehovah's Witnesses, I joined the military—as was legally expected of me. While enlisted, I attended the worship services for the Shincheonji Church (also known by its proper name, Shincheonji Church of Jesus the Temple of the Tabernacles of the Testimony).

Though it is commonly thought by the people of South Korea to be a "cult," I decided to investigate the claims for myself. I spent the next six months studying the Bible for two hours a day and learning of the Shincheonji doctrines. I enjoyed the study and had many questions about their teachings.

In the end, I became uncomfortable with their proselyting techniques. Perhaps because of their unfavorable reputation in South Korea. When they first approached potential investigators, they would not disclose the Church they were from. They also didn't believe in having jobs, saying that working wasn't necessary because the second coming of Christ was so near. After months of studying the movement, I determined that it was not Christ's true Church.

Over the next couple of years, I investigated numerous other religions. I was always sincere, and always looking for the true Church, but I was often disappointed by the fact that none of them were as versed in the Bible as Jehovah's Witnesses were. (I felt that was certainly going to be an earmark of the true Church.) During this period of intensive searching—and when I was twenty-eight years of

I INVESTIGATED **NUMEROUS OTHER RELIGIONS.**

age—I happened upon missionaries from The Church of Jesus Christ of Latter-day Saints. They were also perceived as a "cult" by many people in South Korea, but that never stopped me before, so I began to investigate their Church.

One week after meeting the missionaries, I attended my first LDS sacrament meeting. I also attended the Gospel Principles class. During the lesson, the Spirit brought to my mind a flood of questions I had raised with basically every Church I had investigated: What was the reason for Adam and Eve being cast out for partaking of the fruit? Why kill everyone in Noah's day via the flood? Why is it okay to join the military? What are the qualifications for salvation? What is the role of good works in salvation? What is resurrection? What was the reason for me being born at this time in the history of the world? Obviously I couldn't ask all of these questions during that short Sunday School lesson, but I determined that these questions would be the test I would use to find out if this Church was the true one. If the members did not have answers to these questions, then I would know that this was not God's organization upon the earth.

As I began to meet with the missionaries, attend church, and pray, I found meaningful answers to these questions and many more. I've felt the Spirit in The Church of Jesus Christ of Latter-day Saints in ways that I did not feel it in other churches that I investigated. As would be expected, there are still many things I do not yet know or understand. However, as I continue to study the Church and its doctrines, I continue to find answers to my questions.

One of the great miracles of the gospel has been its influence upon me as a person. It has given me an accurate understanding of God's plan, but it has also provided me with focus and direction—something I struggled to find prior to my conversion. After being baptized, I became a better student. I began to excel both academically and professionally. Upon my conversion, God opened doors for me in my training, employment and even relationships. I was blessed with a rich and abundant life—something I did not have prior to finding the Church. It was all quite remarkable.

I have now been a member of the Church for more than a decade. I have been actively involved in missionary work in the Church, and was sealed to my wife (who is a returned missionary) in the Seoul Korea Temple. The gospel has blessed me personally, and my family specifically, in so many ways. Jesus promised that those who drink of the "living water" will "never thirst" again (see John 4:10 and 14). I have found this to be true. The restored gospel offers this living water, and my thirst is continually quenched by it. The Lord, through His Spirit and His Church, gives me exact answers to my questions and, since joining, I no longer have doubts as to whether or not I am in the church He wants me in. Though my journey was a long one, and I had to search for many years—and through many religions—to find His truth, the effort was worth the tremendous blessings that have come into my life through The Church of Jesus Christ of Latter-day Saints. Finally, I have found a fullness of joy.

THE EFFORT WAS WORTH THE **TREMENDOUS BLESSINGS** THAT HAVE COME INTO MY LIFE THROUGH **THE CHURCH OF JESUS CHRIST OF LATTER-DAY SAINTS.**

KEONGUK

A LESSON TO BE LEARNED

When we think of "enduring to the end" (see Matthew 24:13; 3 Nephi 15:9), we often think of remaining faithful to our testimonies until we pass from this mortal sphere; and that application of Christ's words seems appropriate and applicable. However, in Brother Kim's story we find an additional application of the Book of Mormon's invitation to "press forward, feasting upon the word of Christ, and endure to the end" (2 Nephi 31:20). In Brother Kim's case, the endurance had to do with seeking the truth—in looking for answers to the questions the Spirit continually brought to his mind and heart, but that no church seemed to be able to answer. Keonguk's story is a reminder to each of us that the truth does not come cheap. Christ gave His life for it, as did Peter, Paul, the Prophet Joseph, and a host of others. If the truth of the gospel is worth dying for, it is worth whatever sacrifice that is required to find it, know it, and believe it. Brother Kim's story invites each of us to be willing to pay the price required to know God and to gain a deep and abiding faith in His restored Church.

ALONZO

HINDU

ARUNA PICHHIIKA

I was born into a Hindu family, in Rajahmundry, India. We were very active in the Hindu faith, regularly engaging in puja (or worship) of the various Hindu gods. There are so many gods and goddesses in Hinduism that I did not have one specific god that I worshipped, but there were many that we would make offerings to or pray to. On our visits to the temple, for example, we would offer bananas, coconuts, or other foods to the gods. And, if there were things we were wishing for (or praying for) over a long period of time, and if that wish was granted, we would go to the temple to offer an animal, such as a hen or goat, to give thanks that our prayer had been answered and our request had been granted.

My grandmother used to tell me that there were thirty million gods, and she would tell me the stories of these gods. When we would visit the temples, I would hear these same stories. As I would listen to the various tales about the gods, I used to have lots of doubts about them—and I would wonder to myself, *Did this story really happen? Or is this just a myth?* And so, when

MY GRANDMOTHER USED TO TELL ME THAT THERE WERE THIRTY MILLION GODS.

I was told if I would do this or that, the gods would bless me, I had doubts about what I was being promised. But I was a child and I didn't know, so I followed what I was told—because this is what you do as a child.

Often, in Hinduism, there is a great deal of pressure on the girls to live the religion fully. (There usually isn't that same pressure on the boys to be faithful to Hinduism's tenants and traditions.) The reason so much is expected of the girls is because, after marriage, it is assumed that the girl will teach the children of the traditions and practices of the religion. To do so, she needs to know these tenants thoroughly before becoming a wife

PRACTICING YOUR RELIGION AS A YOUNG GIRL SERVES AS A SORT OF PREPARATION OR TRAINING FOR BEING A WIFE AND A MOTHER IN THE FUTURE.

and a mother in order to carry them on in her new family. Consequently, practicing your religion as a young girl serves as a sort of preparation or training for being a wife and a mother in the future.

The family in which I was raised is large. My mother grew up in a family with seven children, my father in a family of eleven children. When we have family gatherings for puja—such as during an annual festival—all family members from both sides attend. The group is very, very large. When I was about ten or twelve years old, we had one such family gathering for a particular religious holiday. Everyone in the extended family was to be in attendance. My parents fasted for two days prior to the puja and, as part of their preparations, they sat in front of the idols for prolonged periods. Because this was a religious festival, the purpose was to gather, worship, and honor the gods—but my extended family came and spent so much of their time backbiting, gossiping, and fighting instead of worshipping or striving for holiness. As a young girl, this left an impression upon me. I remember thinking to myself, *Why are these people gathering to do the puja, but are not so much worshipping as they are fighting and criticizing each other?* My brother and sister and I were all bothered by this, so we snuck out to escape from all of the negativity and unkindness. This happened year after year.

At one point, my grandmother acquired a serious disease and had to be hospitalized because of it. In an effort to be healed, she was faithful in doing puja and in visiting various Hindu temples, but nothing seemed to work. She did not get well. Indeed, she got worse and worse. She was so sick that she was bedridden and could not speak a word. We were at the hospital one day, after she had been readmitted, waiting outside of her room where she lay near death. While we were waiting to speak with the doctor, a Christian woman—who happened to be in the hospital—made her way into my grandmother's room and she prayed for her. After this prayer, my grandmother fell asleep, and the woman left. While sleeping, my grandmother had a strange dream in which she saw a man wearing a white robe. He had a brightness or glow about him. He gave her something to drink, and told her, "By drinking this, you will be cured." And so, in the dream she saw herself drink what the man had given her. A short time later, after she had awakened from her dream, her doctor visited her in her room and, when he exited the room, he informed the family that somehow our grandmother was healing from the disease that he was quite sure would have taken her life. It took about ten days, but, sure enough, from the time of the dream onward, she steadily improved—and, when she regained her ability to speak, she told us of the dream and the miracle that occurred.

This miracle caused her to have an interest in learning about Jesus and about Christianity; and her failed efforts to be healed by the standard Hindu acts of puja convinced her that those things didn't have the power she had always assumed that they had had. And so, this is how Christianity first came into our family. What's interesting is this: while the miracle of her healing caused her to believe in Christianity, she didn't seek to convert *any* of her family. She let us all continue to practice Hinduism, even though she no longer believed that it had power to heal or save.

SHE **DIDN'T SEEK** TO **CONVERT ANY** OF HER FAMILY.

Because my parents wanted my sister and me to attend a girls-only school, we were enrolled in the only one in the area, which happened to be a Christian school. We didn't really understand anything about Christianity when we started attending there; we simply knew Jesus had been born. However, as we participated in the prayers and hymns each morning, we began to be interested in Jesus and wanted to know more about Him. In time, our puja to the Hindu gods became less and less frequent.

Around this time, my sister and I visited a Christian church unaffiliated with our school. During their worship services, we observed them administering the sacrament, and it was curious to us. We wanted to understand what this ordinance meant for those who participated in it, so we began to ask Christians we knew about it—and that made us very eager to partake. So one day we went to church, and as everyone was in line to partake of the sacrament, we got in line too. When we got to the priest or pastor who was administering it, he could tell we were Hindus because of our bindis—the little red dots we wore on our foreheads. He asked us why we were there and we told him, "You are giving something, and we want to partake of it." He became angry with us and began to yell. We were confused and upset, and so we left. Of course, we never returned to that church. But still, in our hearts we had the feeling that we wanted to partake of the sacrament; and we wondered why we couldn't. We loved

> "YOU ARE **GIVING SOMETHING,** AND WE **WANT TO PARTAKE** OF IT."

Jesus too, so why could we not partake? We just couldn't understand why the priest would withhold it from us.

By this point, we had become all the more interested in Christianity and had lost all interest in Hinduism—in part because of the bad example of our Hindu family members. We had also struggled with the Hindu practice of making offerings of food and money to idols. I remember thinking, *This is a waste. Giving this food to a statue doesn't accomplish anything. Why is the food and money not given to the poor and sick instead? Setting it in front of an idol does not help anyone.*

> GIVING THIS **FOOD** TO A **STATUE** DOESN'T ACCOMPLISH ANYTHING.

Around this same time, my brother was in college. One day he was in a fairly crowded public square there at the university, and he noticed two young Indian men in white shirts with name-tags in their pockets. Of all of the people in this fairly crowded square, the two young men approached my brother and introduced themselves as missionaries of The Church of Jesus Christ of Latter-day Saints. He was shocked. Why had these two young men—who looked very educated and well kept—approached him, and him alone? There were hundreds of people around, and yet they had only approached him. The very fact that they had singled him out piqued his curiosity about them and their message.

> THE VERY FACT THAT THEY HAD **SINGLED HIM OUT** PIQUED HIS **CURIOSITY** ABOUT THEM AND **THEIR MESSAGE.**

They asked for an appointment, and he agreed to meet with them. (As Hindus, we didn't understand that there were different denominations of Christianity. We just assumed all Christians believed the same thing, and were part of the same religion; one God, one Church, one set of beliefs.)

As it approached the day of the appointment, my brother became a bit scared—as he wasn't all that interested in what he assumed the missionaries would share. So he let us know that the missionaries were coming but said he would not be present when they arrived. He said to us, "If you guys are interested, you go ahead and listen to them, but let them know that I am not interested." My sister and I had desperately wanted to better understand Christianity and to partake of the sacrament. We began to think that perhaps God had sent the missionaries specifically to our brother as some sort of a sign. Maybe this was God reaching out to us, trying to show us the path. So we asked our parents if we could listen to the guests when they arrived, and our parents gave us their permission. Our parents actually sat in on the discussion.

As the two elders taught and testified, they were truly inspiring. My sister and I felt a particular spirit as they spoke. Even my parents showed a genuine interest in what they were hearing. And so, after being taught, my parents and my sister and I attended the LDS Church so as to get a better idea of what this new religion was like. The very first time we attended services at the branch, we felt the Lord's Spirit and the peace that we had been lacking in our lives. Even our parents remarked about the Spirit that they felt and their belief that following this Church provided peace in the lives of its members. (They could tell that simply by observing those who were in attendance.) I kept thinking about how when I practiced puja in Hinduism, I didn't feel this peace and the strong spirit I was feeling in the Mormon Church. I did many things as a Hindu in search of that peace, but I never felt it like I felt it here.

Over the next couple of months, we attended church regularly, and we very much enjoyed what we were learning and feeling. However, when the missionaries invited us to be baptized, my parents were shocked. They didn't expect that. They had not thought about becoming Christians. They simply assumed that they would be able to attend and have Jesus as one of their Hindu gods. The invitation to be baptized stunned them, and they declined—telling the elders that they could not be baptized. My parents told the missionaries, "If you're asking us to be baptized, then we can no longer continue. We can come for the worship, but if this leads to baptism, we cannot be a part of it." And so they quit attending church after that, and they no longer met with the missionaries. My sister and I felt terrible.

Though my parents ceased to participate in anything having to do with the Church, my sister and I continued to attend. Before long, we both felt ready to be baptized, but without our parents' support, we could not do so. Over time, we too quit attending. Each morning and each night my sister and I would pray that we could be baptized. We would cry for hours as we held the Book of Mormon and wished to be baptized. The elders had told us, if we prayed, God would speak to us.

WE WOULD **CRY FOR HOURS** AS WE **HELD THE BOOK OF MORMON** AND **WISHED TO BE BAPTIZED.**

So, we would plead, "If you're really there, please speak to us. Guide us. Tell us what we need to do." We finally decided that we simply *had to* be baptized. We *had to* partake of the sacrament. We didn't want to follow idols anymore. But the elders told us that they could not baptize us without our parents' support. So we told them, "Give us six months and we will prove that we can bring our parents to the gospel, because the Lord's Spirit is telling us that our decision to be baptized is correct."

Our parents' concern about us getting baptized was largely wrapped up in the issue of marriage. They were worried that if we became members of the Church, no Hindu man would take us to wife. They did not want our marital options to be limited by choosing (as young single girls) to make a decision that could affect the rest of our lives. We later learned that the sole reason they were unwilling to get baptized themselves was out of fear that it too would adversely affect our marital prospects. The culture and traditions behind marriage in Hindu society are just so ingrained, my parents saw the risk as simply too great. (In Hinduism you have to make arrangements for your children to get married, and you must make an offer to the other family in the form of a dowry. And, in some cases, it is a hard sell. My parents believed we would be less marketable if we were Mormons. How would they get any man and his family to take either of us?) Eventually my parents told the branch president, "President, after our daughters get married, we will join." Of course, my sister and I felt that we needed to put the Lord first, and then He would take care of us. We needed to exercise more faith than our parents were exercising. We cried and prayed more, but our parents were firm in their decision to not let us get baptized.

My sister and I fasted and prayed a lot during this time, and we eventually got baptized without our parents' permission and without their knowledge. We still believed that within six months we could get our parents to accept our baptisms. We pretended that we were not members, but we attended church each week, and our parents were okay with that. They felt that the Church was leading us in the right way, and they were pleased about the influence it was having in our lives, though they had no idea we were already members. Over time, our parents became more involved in the Church and became more withdrawn from Hindu traditions. So once again, the missionaries challenged them to be baptized. This time they were willing to be baptized—though they were still set on my sister and I not being baptized because of its potential influence on our marital prospects. They were baptized, and they became very active in the Church—serving in callings and loving their newfound faith.

About a year later, my sister turned nineteen, and it was standard Hindu age for her to be married. The man that my parents had arranged that she marry served in a temple dedicated to the Hindu

IT WAS **TIME TO TELL OUR PARENTS** THAT **WE HAD BEEN BAPTIZED.**

god, Vishnu. When my sister and I realized what was happening, we became scared. We were baptized members of the Church. How could she marry a Hindu worshipper of Vishnu? So we rushed to the Church to talk to the branch president. He suggested that it was time to tell our parents that we had been baptized, but we were so afraid. The mission president happened to be visiting the branch that day, and so we spoke with him about how my sister was expected to marry this Vishnu worshipper, and that she didn't want to. He listened to my sister, and then asked, "Would you be interested in going on a mission?" (That was certainly one way to deal with an unwanted marriage proposal.) The mission president didn't realize that our parents did not know that we were members. When he discovered that we had kept this from our parents, he informed us that we *must* talk with our parents and let them know that we had been baptized members of the Church.

We came to the decision that the branch president and mission president were right. We knew we needed to tell our parents. We felt that day that, whatever the consequences of our choices, we were ready to die for Christ. We had accepted Jesus. Indeed, we had accepted Him *before* the other members of our family, and we couldn't hold that in anymore. And we couldn't live as Hindus anymore. So, my sister and I took a picture of us—taken on the day we were baptized, all dressed in white—and we presented it to our mother. She was so confused by it. She asked, "Why are you guys wearing baptismal clothes? Tell me what has happened! What did you do? Tell me! Did you get baptized?" When we admitted that we had, she screamed and cried and cried. She was certain that our chance for marriage was ruined. She grabbed us and, crying, said, "How could you take such a big step without our knowledge? Baptism is a sacred thing. It is not for a child to decide. It is sacred!" In Hinduism, if you're not following the traditions of the faith, many feel the gods will punish you. My mother worried—not just about our ability to get married—but that we might have provoked the wrath of God by joining the Church when we were not spiritually mature enough to faithfully live our covenants. We assured her, "Don't worry, Mom. God will take care of us."

Well, our mother was very distraught about how my father and brother might react to the news that the two of us had been baptized. As she told them about our conversion, my sister and I were shocked to learn that our brother had also been baptized—though we were unaware of that. So, here

A **FAMILY** OF **FIVE**— ALL **MEMBERS** OF THE **CHURCH,** BUT ALL **ASSUMING** THAT THE **OTHERS WERE NOT MEMBERS** YET.

we were—a family of five—all members of the Church, but all assuming that the others were not members yet. My parents and brother thought my sister and I were still Hindu, and my sister and I thought my brother was still a Hindu. But *everyone* was already a member!

We thought our father would be so very angry because of all of this, but he had such a big smile on his face that we felt like freed birds! My brother and father were thrilled for us and comforted our mother—who was still quite devastated. I remember them saying, "Don't worry! They have strong faith and strong testimonies. God will take care of them. Don't worry!"

In 2001, my sister served a mission and in 2002, my brother served a mission. In 2003, I served a mission also. This made my parents so happy, and my mission was such a blessing in my life. I learned so much. I gained a deeper understanding of the gospel, of people, of responsibility, and so on.

As we each served our missions and then returned and married in the temple, my parents' testimonies increased. We had told them that the Lord would take care of us if we had faith in Him. You must put God first in your life and then you can trust that He will take care of everything else. Well, He proved that to my parents. When my sister got married in the temple, they no longer worried about me and my prospects for marriage. They truly believed that God would bless me as He had our entire family since our conversions—and He has!

When our extended family begin to learn that each of us were serving missions, they came to my parents and asked what was going on. "Are you becoming Christians?" they asked. "Are you believing in Jesus Christ? Are you going to church?" I wondered how my parents would handle this, but they responded with boldness, "Yes! Yes, we are Christians! We are now going to the Mormon Church!" Their testimonies had made them so strong. We had accepted Jesus Christ. We had accepted the Book of Mormon—which we believe is another testament of Jesus Christ. The Lord had showed us the way, and this was the fullness of the gospel. Because we believed this, we could not live as Hindus anymore. To this day, my parents give this same testimony to anyone who asks them if they have left Hinduism. They are so happy in the Church!

One additional thing that played a role in our conversion to the gospel was how we were treated when we visited the Church. In our process of finding the gospel, we had interactions with various churches and Christians. A priest yelled at us for trying to take the sacrament. Another Christian rebuked us for wearing a bindi. Someone else was critical because we had attended the worship services of a particular denomination. I remember thinking, *Why are they acting this way? Jesus is the same for everyone. Why are Christian people treating others like this?* But when we came to The Church of Jesus Christ of Latter-day Saints, people never said to us, "Why are you wearing a bindi?" Or "Why are you doing this?" or "Why are you doing that?" They did not say anything about our Hindu customs or traditions, but they accepted us with an open heart. They accepted us for who we were.

Trials will come. Build your testimony upon the Rock! Trust Jesus! He will lead you right. Once you take the first step, don't turn back again. Seek to help others have the wonderful blessings God has given you. And be proud to say, "We are the Mormons!"

BE **PROUD** TO SAY, "WE ARE THE MORMONS!"

ARUNA

A LESSON TO BE LEARNED

Since at least as early as 1718, English speakers have used the phrase "a perfect storm" to reference an unusual coming together of events that bring to pass some unexpected result. Aruna's conversion seems to be exactly that. A number of things played a role in her conversion, including: doubts about the Hindu gods, the bad example of family members, the miraculous healing of her grandmother, attending a Christian girls' school, a chance meeting of Mormon missionaries by her brother, an arranged marriage for her sister, and undeniable feelings of the Spirit. All of these things combined led to her conversion to Christ and His Church.

Elder Neal A. Maxwell of the Twelve reminded the Saints, "God is in the details of our lives."[1] On another occasion, he stated, "A universal God is actually involved with our small, individual universe of experience! In the midst of His vast dominions, yet He numbers us, knows us, and loves us perfectly."[2] Aruna's conversion is a testament to the reality that, as immeasurable as God's dominions are, He knows each of us intimately, is involved in the details of our lives, and will bring to pass the "perfect storm" in order to facilitate our conversion to Christ and His gospel.

ALONZO

NOTES

1. Neal A. Maxwell, "Becoming a Disciple," *Ensign*, June 1996.
2. Neal A. Maxwell, "'Yet Thou Art Here,'" *Ensign*, November 1987.

JEHOVAH'S WITNESS

LEE NOBLEMAN

Latter-day Saints and Jehovah's Witnesses are two of the most zealous and committed Christian denominations—each sure that *their brand* of Christianity is the "only true" one and each willing to do whatever it takes to spread the word. Thus, going from Witness to Mormon was a bumpy ride and not an easy transition to make. However, God opened my eyes—which I had tried so desperately to squeeze shut—and thereby He allowed me to see the light.

My conversion really started in 1988, when my girlfriend and I visited a high school friend of ours who happened to be one of Jehovah's Witnesses. Neither of us were aware of her religious affiliation at the time, but what I would learn that day in her kitchen would change the course of my life.

GOD OPENED MY EYES— WHICH I HAD TRIED SO DESPERATELY TO SQUEEZE SHUT—AND THEREBY HE ALLOWED ME TO SEE THE LIGHT.

I remember the three of us—all recent high school graduates—sitting around the kitchen table discussing the impeachment of the controversial Arizona Governor, Evan Mecham. In the middle of our conversation, my friend's father entered the room and joined in our discussion. I remember asking him something like, "Did you vote for Mecham?" His reply surprised me: "We're Jehovah's Witnesses. We don't vote, run for office, salute the flag, or engage in politics *in any way*. Our allegiance is to Jehovah—God, not to an earthly kingdom or mortal ruler." I had never heard of such a thing. I was fascinated and puzzled at the same time, and I wanted to hear more. When I began to intently ask him question after question, he offered to come over to my apartment with a brother from their congregation and tell me more about the Witnesses. I enthusiastically agreed—and we set a date and time to start our Bible study together.

I suppose there were several reasons why I was so interested in his unique beliefs. I was certainly drawn in by the distinctiveness of this man's theology, but I was also motivated to learn more by the fact that I had, from my childhood, been interested in spiritual things. That was just a natural part of who I was. Religion was something that readily piqued my interest—and, as religions go, the Witnesses have one of the most curious theologies. So I readily accepted the invitation to learn more.

I was raised as an Episcopalian and, as a kid, I attended a private Catholic school in Philadelphia. I had Jewish relatives—I myself being a descendent of Ashkenazi Jews. I also lived in a neighborhood fairly saturated with Jews and, consequently, I had been exposed quite heavily to the Jewish tradition. I will admit, however, as an active Episcopalian, I had my struggles with Christianity. There seemed to be so many competing doctrines, philosophies, and practices; I was at a loss as to how to tell which was right and which was wrong. I wasn't sure how to know which things were the teachings of

> THERE SEEMED TO BE SO MANY **COMPETING DOCTRINES, PHILOSOPHIES, AND PRACTICES;** I WAS **AT A LOSS** AS TO HOW TO TELL **WHICH WAS RIGHT AND WHICH WAS WRONG.**

men, and which were of God. I suppose, in many ways, I was like young Joseph, who asked a similar question, and who expressed his concern that, "so great were the confusion and strife among the different denominations, that it was impossible for a person young as I was, and so unacquainted with men and things, to come to any certain conclusion who was right and who was wrong" (JS—H 1:8). This well captures my own sentiment at the time.

While I wasn't sure about this doctrine or that doctrine, I did know enough from my Episcopalian days to argue rather effectively with my evangelical acquaintances who had a propensity to preach hell-fire, judgment, and damnation—but didn't seem to radiate much of the love of Christ. This bothered me greatly. You've got various people and groups going around saying that their view of God and religion is the "right one," and yet so many of them manifest so little love. I assumed that a group that had the "truth" would also reflect that, not just in their doctrine, but also in their spirit and demeanor. From the scriptures, I felt I had a pretty good sense of the personality of Christ, but from my interaction with various churches, I didn't see much of it in the people who were their representatives.

Well, a week or so after first meeting my Witness friend's father, he (and another man) arrived at my apartment for our Bible study. After we had exchanged pleasantries, one of them asked me if I believed in the Trinity. As a practicing Episcopalian, I proudly said, "Yes!" (Of course, they expected that.) One of them quickly followed up with another question: "Can you explain the Trinity to us?" Again, as an active attendee of my Church, I felt confident that I could. I took a deep breath, opened my mouth, and suddenly realized I had no idea how to explain this most central of Episcopalian doctrines. I had heard the Trinity referenced over and over

I HAD **NO IDEA** HOW TO **EXPLAIN** THIS **MOST CENTRAL** OF EPISCOPALIAN **DOCTRINES.**

again throughout my childhood and adolescence, but I never took the time to really contemplate it—or to make sure that I understood it. In addition, I had no idea that there were different versions of the Trinity: Modalists (who think the Father, Son, and Holy Spirit are one person with the equivalent of three costumes), Psychological Trinitarians (who think the Trinity is one God with basically three different personalities), Social Trinitarians (who believe that the Father, Son, and Holy Spirit are three distinct persons whose relationship constitutes one God), etc. Until my conversation with my Witness acquaintances, I had always assumed everyone who believed in the Trinity believed the same thing. Of course, what that "same thing" was I had just proven I did not know! But, whatever it was I believed, I assumed all Christians believed the same.

As I thought through what I believed about God, I found myself uncomfortable with the notion that God the Father and Jesus where the same person. That didn't feel right. However, as I realized that there was so much confusion among the various denominations of Christianity on such a central tenet, I suddenly found myself questioning whether or not Christianity was actually true. Fortunately, sensing my dismay, these two good men opened the Bible and shared with me what the scriptures had to say about the nature of God.

In my conversations with Jehovah's Witnesses, I came to learn that much of what traditional Christianity teaches is not scripturally based—but has crept into the Christian Church over the centuries and is a consequence of councils and Hellenization. As would be expected, I began to call into question the faith of my fathers.

In the ensuing days, weeks, and months, I regularly met with my Witness friends. I also continued to intently read and study on my own. Eventually—after two years of intense learning—I was baptized one of Jehovah's Witnesses. I became an active "publisher"—which is the title Witnesses use for those who go door-to-door sharing the "Truth." (I spent about thirty hours a week in active proselyting.)

Through the process of my conversion to the Witness faith and doctrine, I came to a firm belief that the scriptures are from God, and that they literally contain the word of God. I became convinced that God had an authorized "organization" upon the earth, and that the Watchtower Bible and Tract Society was that "organization." I also began to believe that we were living in the end of this "system of things"—as Witnesses say; that God was about to destroy all of the false organized religions that populated this earth. Finally, I developed faith in the love of God and Jesus and decided to swear my eternal allegiance to Them, and to no one or nothing else. And so, for the next twelve years I was an active, proselyting Witness of Jehovah—God.

FOR THE NEXT **TWELVE YEARS** I WAS AN ACTIVE, **PROSELYTING WITNESS OF JEHOVAH**—GOD.

Fast forward more than a decade. One afternoon there was a knock on my front door. When I opened it, I discovered a pair of LDS missionaries with broad smiles standing on my doorstep. I invited them in, but it was not what I would call a cordial meeting. They taught, and I firmly refuted their teachings. They left, never to return. In retrospect, I feel bad about what occurred. But they had knocked on the door of a committed Witness. I certainly wasn't going to miss an opportunity to teach and testify to my young, misinformed friends.

A few months later there was another knock on the door. This time I was greeted by sisters, rather than elders. I discovered that I lived in an apartment that had apparently been previously occupied by a less-active Latter-day Saint family, and the missionaries were out looking for members who had "gone off the grid," so to speak. Hence the two visits in such a short window of time.

As with the elders, I invited the sister missionaries in. I suppose I was a bit better behaved this time—but only just. Once again, we spoke, we argued, and we were largely unproductive. However, they came back—and we became friends. And, over time, I found myself developing respect for the missionaries and also for the members of the LDS Church. And, even though I felt their knowledge of the Bible was sorely lacking, I could not deny the goodness of the people I had met.

By way of confession, I have to admit that I allowed them into my home—and spent months discussing their religion—not because I was looking for something I felt I was lacking, but really for two other reasons. First, I thought I could convert them, and I was up for the challenge. (Clearly they were thinking the same thing about me!) Second, Jehovah's Witness literature often provides information for its members on other religions; but there was almost *nothing* in the literature about the Mormons. That struck me as strange—*very strange*—and so I was curious to know a bit more about what Mormons believe.

You often hear of missionaries who challenge their investigators to be baptized the very first time they meet. This wasn't the approach the missionaries used with me. On the contrary, they took things very slowly with me. We moved methodically from one discussion to the next, and I agreed with very little of what they shared. After months of them teaching and me disagreeing, one of the sisters asked me if I would "follow the example set by Jesus and be baptized." I burst out laughing because the question was absurd—so absurd, I thought it was a joke! I kept laughing for some time until I realized *I was the only one laughing.* Sister Bonny, who had asked the question, was now openly crying. I quickly apologized and told the sisters that, while I greatly respected them, after talking to them for months I was more certain than ever that *I* had the truth. Their efforts to teach me had only convinced me more that my Church was true and theirs was not. In addition, how could I be baptized when we agreed on *nothing*! Sister Bonny excused herself and ran to the bathroom. Her companion quickly followed after but first took the time to tell me that I was a "jerk." While there was very little the sisters had taught me that I could agree with, unfortunately, they were right about this—*I was a jerk!*

UNFORTUNATELY, THEY WERE RIGHT ABOUT THIS—I WAS A JERK!

After what seemed like an eternity, the two sister missionaries came out of the bathroom, gathered their things, and prepared to leave. But just prior to leaving, Sister Bonny turned to me and bore her testimony. Her companion did likewise. I was absolutely overwhelmed! I had been active in the Witness faith for some twelve years, but I can honestly say that this was the first time I could remember *ever* feeling the Spirit. It came with such power and certainty that I could not dismiss it. Indeed, I was in awe at the force and certainty of the missionaries' testimonies. And yet, how could these young women be *so sure* when they struggled *so much* to support from the Bible the most basic of LDS doctrines? It made no sense to me. And yet, oddly enough, I was no longer sure I had all of the answers. Thirty minutes ago I *knew* that I was right and that they were *totally* wrong. Now I stood in front of two twenty-two-year-old girls, and I knew they knew more than I did.

I STOOD IN FRONT OF TWO TWENTY-TWO-YEAR-OLD GIRLS, AND I KNEW THEY KNEW MORE THAN I DID.

The sisters took their things and left; and I immediately found myself doing some serious soul searching. How many things had I dismissed that I now needed to go back and—*for the first time*—sincerely listen to and consider? How many things had my arrogance prevented me from hearing? As the thoughts flooded my mind, I had to confess that the LDS Church, as an international religion, was eagerly engaged in bringing the gospel truth to any who were willing to listen. (As a Witness, this was something of paramount importance to me—and something I largely assumed no one other than the Witnesses was doing.) I suddenly realized that the message of the Mormons was united and clear—something most Christian denominations could not claim. And, more importantly, the people matched their message. They were the epitome of the description Christ gave of His faithful followers. I suddenly knew that I needed to know more. I realized that I needed to shut up and listen; I needed to actually try to understand what they were teaching, instead of just trying to refute every little thing they said. I called the sisters and invited them back, asking if we could start over again. And we did.

We started from square one. They taught me what they had taught me before, but I actually listed this time—not only with my ears, but also with my heart. Many months passed, and I eventually joined The Church of Jesus Christ of Latter-day Saints. I have to admit, I didn't want to. I suppose that stubborn part of me still didn't want to acknowledge that for so many years I believed something that wasn't true—and I taught that inaccurate view of the gospel to many, many people. So I struggled to humble myself sufficiently to want to be baptized, but I did it out of obedience to my Father.

Truth be told, beyond stubbornness, one of the things that made conversion so hard was the fear of having to walk away from all of my friends, from all of the people and things that

I WAS GOING TO **LOSE** A LOT TO **EMBRACE** WHAT I FELT I HAD **GAINED.**

had, for so many years, given my life meaning and direction. Learning that I had been wrong in by beliefs was like having the rug pulled out from beneath me, and it didn't just require a change in my doctrinal beliefs—it required a complete change in my life. I was going to lose a lot to embrace what I felt I had gained. Just gaining a testimony was a grueling process, but this next step would take a great deal of faith. As would be expected, when I told the elders who presided over the Witness congregation I attended that I was joining the LDS Church, they indicated that I was in a state of apostasy—and I was disfellowshipped (which is the Witness term for excommunicated). Those who had been my closest friends now shunned me, and I was completely cut off. It was so very painful. I lost a great deal of weight—I suppose because of the stress—and I was, in many ways, devastated. But, gratefully, with the support of the many missionaries who had taught me, along with the help of the amazing members of my ward, I was able to muster the faith to embrace what I now knew to be true.

In Douglas Adams's classic novel, *The Hitchhikers Guide to the Galaxy*,[1] a group of hyper-intelligent pan-dimensional beings inquire of a supercomputer, named "Deep Thought," what "the answer to the ultimate question of life, the universe, and everything" is. The computer informs them that the answer to the meaning of everything is "forty-two." Deep Thought points out that the answer seems meaningless because the beings who instructed him never actually knew what the question was. The profundity of this episode should not be missed. First of all, I spent years giving the answers, but I really didn't understand the questions. Second, in the process, I discovered that forty-two was *not* the answer to the meaning of everything. No, not forty-two! But Jesus did give the answer. In the Gospel of John, He explained to His apostles how one could recognize His *true* followers. He said, "By this shall all men know that ye are my disciples, if ye have love one to another" (John 13:35). Love; love is the answer to *everything*—including the question, "Which Church is true?" In my process of conversion, I discovered something more than simply my Church was wrong and their Church was right. I discovered that there had been something I had been missing during all my years of active church participation. I hadn't really been able to put my finger on it up until this point. But now I noticed it, and it made all of the difference. With no intention to be critical, and in acknowledging all of the very impressive things about the members of the Watchtower Bible and Tract Society, what was lacking was *love*. I didn't feel God's love, and I didn't learn as a Witness to convey that love. It's from love that all of the other fruits of the Spirit come, and without love, they have

> I HAD LEARNED TO BE **MORE CONCERNED** ABOUT **BEING RIGHT** THAN I WAS ABOUT **LIVING RIGHT.**

no source from which to spring forth. Please know that none of this is to imply that there are not loving people within the Kingdom Halls, but the perfect bond of union in the scriptures is love. As individuals, many are filled with great love—but the organization of which I was a part for so many years was lacking it. I had learned to be more concerned about being right than I was about living right—about loving others, particularly those who did not know the truth. Somehow, I had never noticed that when you read the Bible, you never see Jesus in a bash! He pointed out false doctrine but did so in love and compassion. He couldn't tolerate hypocrisy, but He was quite tolerant of those who simply had wrong theological ideas. Jesus wanted people to see the truth—but that truth was less about how far you could walk on the Sabbath or whether you should pay your taxes. The ultimate truth of Jesus was love: teaching out of love, ministering out of love, forgiving out of love. He was void of pride and arrogance and taught his true disciples that they should be the same. He had compassion on, and manifest love for, those who were simply doctrinally deceived. He didn't loathe them, and He didn't bash with them, but He certainly loved them! And yet, that was not who I was, nor was it the message of my movement.

As I look back on my life prior to my conversion to The Church of Jesus Christ of Latter-day Saints, I feel much as Paul must have on the road to Damascus, determined and certain until blinded with almost overwhelming purity. For Paul, that purity came in the form of the resurrected Lord, but for me, it came in the form of a testimony borne by two valiant daughters of our God. Like Paul, after my brush with the light, I was dependent on the members for help and, like the Apostle of old, I too needed them to forgive and forget the old me. The one who stood by and stoned Stephen was a new creation born of God's love, as am I. While I like to think my story is unique, I think the basics are universal. If the missionaries had chosen to act like I did—to argue instead of bearing their testimonies—and if the members hadn't embraced me and loved me regardless of my argumentative nature, I would have continued to "kick against the pricks" (Acts 9:5), as Paul had.

No! Forty-two is *not* the Answer! *Love* is the Answer!

LEE

A LESSON TO BE LEARNED

The key to conversion in this story is quite clear: it was love! President Thomas S. Monson asked, "Do our human relations reflect the spirit of love?" He then pointed out, "He that loveth his fellow men can lead them to God. . . . Love is the catalyst that causes change. Love is the balm that brings healing to the soul. But love doesn't grow like weeds or fall like rain. Love has its price."[2] We must work hard to ensure that others know of our sincere love for them. That love must be rooted in godly care, not in the sole desire to convert our non-LDS friends.

Just as love can lead those we know to God and to the Church, the reverse is also true. The Book of Mormon is quite clear that the bad example of the members can cause nonmembers to reject the gospel (for example, Alma 4:10–12, 39:11), and it can also cause those who are in the Church to lose their faith and leave. Our interactions with others must be loving and unconditional. Such a demeanor among the members will do more to cause the Church to grow than will any number of full-time missionaries.

ALONZO

NOTES

1. Douglas Adams, *The Hitchhiker's Guide to the Galaxy* (New York: Random House, Inc., 2009).
2. Thomas S. Monson, *Teachings of Thomas S. Monson*, comp. Lynne F. Cannegieter (Salt Lake City: Deseret Book, 2011), 173–74.

JUDAISM

MITCH COWITZ

I was born into an observant Jewish family, the only son of my parents' four children. I am a second generation Canadian, being a descendant of Polish Jews who emigrated from Drildz (Ilza) and Apt (Opatow)—located in southeast Poland. Like many other Jews, my family members who did not flee Eastern Europe died in Nazi concentration camps during the Second World War.

Judaism has a number of denominations: the Haredi (or ultra-Orthodox), modern Orthodox, Conservative, and Reformed. I was raised in a traditional Conservative Jewish family. The Conservative movement considers itself "mainstream" Judaism. Whereas the Orthodox Jews are strictly observant of the Torah, and Reformed Jews are often not strongly committed to many of the traditional Jewish customs and practices, Conservative Jews are middle-of-the-road Jews, caught halfway between tradition and modernity. Thus, in the home in which I was raised, we kept a kosher table—and we maintained separate dishes, cutlery, and pots for milk and meat. We believed the Torah was binding on our day-to-day lives, but we believed in modern innovations. (For example, we believed that it was okay to drive our car on the Sabbath.) As a family, we commemorated the various feast and festivals of Judaism—Rosh Hashanah,

Yom Kippur, the Passover, and so forth. I had a very traditional Jewish upbringing and my faith was central to who I was.

Dedicated to their faith, as my parents were, they wanted my sisters and me to have a sound Jewish education and so I attended a private Hebrew school throughout my childhood and preteen years. There I studied all facets of Jewish history and culture, as well as the Torah and the Hebrew language. Most of the kids in the school I attended were Orthodox, and yet I felt at home, and my love for and faith in Judaism grew during those years. I attended the synagogue weekly and lived my religion faithfully. At the age of thirteen, I had my Bar Mitzvah—the traditional Jewish rite of passage where one is officially acknowledged to be a man. I even went on a trip to Israel at that time. I was, by all accounts, a very traditional Jew.

The neighborhood in Toronto where I grew up was predominately Jewish, and all of my friends and associates during those years were practicing Jews. This really served to reinforce my beliefs, and I never really considered the fact that there were people of different religions out there. Indeed, it wasn't until I attended a public high school that I started to associate with people of other faiths. Of course, that would play a role in my eventual conversion to the gospel.

> I **NEVER REALLY CONSIDERED** THE FACT THAT THERE WERE **PEOPLE OF DIFFERENT RELIGIONS** OUT THERE.

Even though we lived in a very Jewish neighborhood, we did have some neighbors who lived across the street from us who were Latter-day Saint Christians. (How they landed in a predominantly Jewish neighborhood, I do not know.) The kids in their family were a bit older than I was, but I got to know them and, on several occasions, they talked to me about Jesus Christ. At one point my parents became aware of this, and went over to their home to have a conversation about this with their parents. From that time on, at least for the next few years, we didn't speak to each other.

As a child, I had heard a fair amount about Jesus—mostly from television or radio. I wouldn't say that I had a good understanding of Christianity or of what Jesus taught, but I had heard enough to be curious—and to wonder why Jews didn't accept Him as the Messiah. What

I had heard didn't make me want to be a Christian, and it didn't make me believe in Jesus. But it was sufficient to make me curious about what the Jewish position on Jesus was and how we dealt with the fact that a Jewish man claimed to be God's son. At around eleven or twelve years of age I asked my father about this, but he gave me an answer that didn't fully satisfy me. He simply said that Paul conjured up this notion that Jesus was the Messiah, even though he really wasn't. In so many words, my father argued that

> ## HE SIMPLY SAID THAT PAUL CONJURED UP THIS NOTION THAT JESUS WAS THE MESSIAH, EVEN THOUGH HE REALLY WASN'T.

Paul took the Jesus of history and turned Him into the Christ of the Bible. I thought that was interesting, but somehow it didn't really answer the lingering questions that I had about Jesus, Christianity, and Judaism's position on these matters of history.

A number of years later (in 1985), when I was enrolled in college in Toronto and studying radio broadcasting, I had a class assignment to track down a particular album—and I knew my Mormon neighbors had it. So I approached them and asked if they would like to help me with the assignment I was working on. They accepted my request and, in the process of working on the project together, we became quite close.

As I noted, we had grown up together, and they would occasionally talk to me about Christianity and about their Church. Of course, as I've pointed out, this upset my parents; but I also really wanted no part of it. I was a Jew. Stop talking to me about Christianity! I really disliked their tendency to be so aggressive in their proselyting.

Once we had become friends again, my LDS neighbors would regularly talk about "the pageant." I heard them reference it enough that I finally asked them, "What is this 'pageant' you're always talking about?" They told me that it was a play held in upper-state New York each year, and was called "The Hill Cumorah Pageant." They said it was performed on the side of a large hill, and that the play told the story of the American Indians. Since Palmyra, New York, was only about three and a half hours from where we lived, they asked if I would be interested in driving down to see the play. Of course, there is quite a bit of Native American history in the eastern portion of North America. "Toronto" is a Native American word meaning "where there are trees in water." Even the word "Canada" is from a Huron-Iroquois root word that means "settlement" or "village." So the story of the Native Americans was the historical foundation of the area in which I was raised, and the idea of seeing a play that talked about such things sounded very interesting to me. Consequently, one Saturday afternoon we piled into my mother's car, and we all drove to Palmyra to learn about the "American Indians." As we drove up to the site where the pageant was held, I saw a very large sign, which read: "America's Witness for Christ: The Hill Cumorah Pageant. The Church of Jesus Christ of Latter-day Saints." I began to realize that I had been tricked. I was not happy that my LDS neighbors hadn't been truthful with me. This was clearly a Church production of some kind and, being Jewish, I wanted no part of it. When I objected, they told me to just relax and watch the play. (To be fair, I should point out that at that time they weren't very active Mormons. And so I'm not exactly sure that they understood that lying was not the best way to share the gospel. Regardless, even in their inactivity, they were being missionaries. So who can fault them?)

Reluctantly, I *did* watch the play; and I felt something. I felt that what I had just watched must have some truth in it. This wasn't an intellectual conclusion; it was a spiritual one,

THIS WAS CLEARLY A CHURCH PRODUCTION OF SOME KIND AND, BEING JEWISH, I WANTED NO PART OF IT.

based on the strong feelings I had experienced during the pageant. At that time, I really didn't understand anything about the Holy Ghost and certainly didn't realize that that was what I was feeling. I simply knew that I had felt something strong, and whatever that feeling was, it caused me to believe that what I had been taught at the Hill Cumorah was true. This was a major turning point in the process of my conversion.

Oddly, as an observant Jew, one would think that this would cause me a significant amount of cognitive dissidence, but somehow it didn't. Because I had felt the Spirit's confirmation, things started to fall into place intellectually, and what I had learned about Jesus's visit to the Americas and the coming forth of the Book of Mormon began to make sense to me.

After staying in a hotel that night, we visited some Church history sites, including the Sacred Grove, the E. B. Grandin building, and the

Peter Whitmer farm. We spent most of the day visiting and learning about these sights so sacred to the Restoration. When the time came where we needed to go back home, I didn't want to leave. (As we had visited these sights, I had continued to feel that same Spirit I had first encountered during the pageant, and my conversion only deepened with each Church property we visited.)

My LDS friends had spoken frequently about the Church's temple in Washington, D.C. (The Toronto temple had yet to be built at this point.) Prior to this trip to Palmyra, I can't say that I was that curious about the LDS temple. However, now that I had experienced all that I had at the other Church history sites, I just had to see the temple. So we piled back into the car and drove to D.C.

My friends had told me that modern-day temples are "fashioned after Solomon's temple." I had learned a lot about Solomon's temple in Hebrew school, so I had a pretty good idea of what to expect. Once again, I found that my somewhat inactive LDS friends were not totally accurate in their description. Nevertheless, we drove to D.C. and spent the week at the visitors' center (next to the temple), learning more about the Church and the role the temples play in it.

Though I didn't think much about the consequences of all of this while I was with my friends in New York, I knew that when I arrived home this was going to cause problems. Upon returning to my parents' house, my family thought I had joined a "cult." I had actually *not* joined the Church at

MY FAMILY THOUGHT I HAD JOINED A "CULT."

this point, but there was such a noticeable change in my countenance that my parents and other relatives could tell that something had happened to me. I remember my brother-in-law saying to me, "Get that look off your face!" I said, "What look?" And he replied, "Your whole countenance has changed." I had a glow about me that was a result of the things I had learned and, I suppose, a consequence of the fact that I was not fighting—but embracing what the Spirit was revealing to me.

I had left Toronto a committed Jew—who was put off by the proselyting of Christians—and had returned home a believer in the restored gospel of Jesus Christ. I had gained a testimony at the Hill Cumorah Pageant. Ironically, I had not prayed about it—or about the Book of

Mormon. I just knew it was true. I just knew! And to this day, I *know* it to be true!

Investigators are encouraged to apply "Moroni's Promise" (Moroni 10:3–5), but I simply had not had a chance to do so, since I hadn't even read the Book of Mormon yet. While we were on our trip, I obtained my first copy of the Book of Mormon and would soon throw myself into a study of it, but it simply didn't play a role in my initial testimony. That had come independent of all of the traditional components—praying, reading the Book of Mormon, attending Church, taking the missionary discussions and so forth.

I knew I had to be baptized—and I desperately wanted to be—but I was too afraid of what my family would do if I actually joined. I had every expectation that they would kick me out, disown me, and never speak to me again, so I postponed getting baptized for two more years. During that time, I continued to celebrate the Jewish holidays with my family, but I ceased to attend the synagogue. Though I didn't attend sacrament meeting weekly during the next two years, I did watch LDS general conference and attend the occasional fireside—and I also read the Book of Mormon, Doctrine and Covenants, New Testament, *A Marvelous Work and a Wonder*,[1] *Jesus the Christ*,[2] and many more books—as I sought the courage to tell my parents that I wanted to be baptized into the LDS Church. After two years, I finally mustered the courage to let my parents know that I was going to become a Latter-day Saint. As I expected, their response was visceral, to say the least. They did everything *but* disown me. They cut me off financially, and our relationship was quite strained because of my conversion. During this time, I felt much like Joseph. When confronted by those who persecuted him for saying that he had seen a vision, he wrote (in his personal history), "I knew it, and I knew that God knew it, and I could not deny it, neither dared I do it; at least I knew that by so doing I would offend God, and come under condemnation" (JS—H 1:25). This was exactly how I felt. God had given me a witness of the Restoration. I knew that he had.

And, with Joseph, I had to ask myself, "Who am I that I can withstand God, or why does the world think to make me deny what I have actually" experienced? (JS—H 1:25). I had a testimony, and I knew I needed to act on that—regardless of the adverse consequences that doing so might bring into my life.

I was finally baptized on July 4, 1987, and I have no regrets about making that decision. While it has strained the relationship I have with my parents and siblings, it has also brought into my life so many blessings and so much joy, chief among them a beautiful wife and two wonderful children to whom I am sealed for time and all eternity. It has also brought me a knowledge of the Atonement of Jesus Christ and an understanding of my ability to be forgiven when I fall short. This knowledge brings me great peace. The Book of Mormon has also been a tremendous blessing in my life. It talks a great deal about the Jews—and, from the time I began reading it, I felt like it was *my book*. I felt as though I was reading a record of *my* ancestors. The gospel has also provided me with a testimony of modern prophets. Who can place a price on the inspired counsel of prophets, seers, and revelators?

One of the things that has helped me to endure the trials brought about because of my conversion has been my knowledge, not only of God's love for me, but also of the reality that He has a plan for me—and that my conversion was part of that greater plan for my life. That knowledge has enabled me to endure the rejection of family members and the strained relationships caused by me embracing Jesus Christ and His gospel. My conversion brought me a conviction that God is in this work. I don't simply *believe* the Church is true; I *know* it is.

None of this is to suggest that becoming a Latter-day Saint has required that I reject my past and who I am. If anything, the gospel has encouraged me to bring all of the truth and good that Judaism taught me and to simply add to that the further light and knowledge the restored gospel offers. Thus, when I am with my parents and siblings around the Jewish holidays, I still commemorate those events with them, and many parts of Judaism have made their way into the raising of my children. My religious past colors my faith today—as it should. I still

"I AM **JEWISH BY BIRTH, BUT CHRISTIAN BY FAITH.**"

consider myself Jewish—and always will. And when people ask me about my conversion, I typically say: "I am Jewish by birth, but Christian by faith."

If I were to try to draw a lesson from my conversion, I suppose it would be this: follow the Spirit. Obey its counsel when it tells you to do something difficult. Follow its promptings when it inspires you to say or do something. Believe its witness when it testifies to you of truth. No matter how inconvenient those promptings are, follow them . . . obey them. That's where the blessings are to be found. That's where God's power to lead and direct your life will come in.

> NO MATTER HOW **INCONVENIENT** THOSE **PROMPTINGS** ARE, **FOLLOW THEM … OBEY THEM.**

MITCH

A LESSON TO BE LEARNED

Life is filled with paradoxes, and while we would not typically celebrate a wrong, we must acknowledge that wrong choices sometimes play into God's hands. Judas facilitated the death of Jesus and, thereby, enabled the Atonement to happen. Conspiring men slew the prophet Joseph, thereby enabling him to seal his testimony with his blood—something God had deemed necessary (see D&C 136:39).

In Mitch's story, his conversion was ultimately facilitated by a little "white lie"—by an invitation from his semi-active Latter-day Saint friends to an event that was not as they had billed it. It is ever true that two wrongs do not make a right. However, it is also true that God can turn any number of wrongs into something right if He needs to. What could have caused Mitch to reject the gospel ultimately led to his embracing it. Perhaps the greatest threat to God's work are the members, because of our tremendous weaknesses and imperfections. Thankfully, the Father moves the work forward in spite of us—and because He so deeply loves each of His children.

ALONZO

NOTES

1. LeGrand Richards, *A Marvelous Work and a Wonder* (Salt Lake City: Deseret Book, 1976).
2. James E. Talmage, *Jesus the Christ* (Salt Lake City: Deseret Book, 1982).

MUSLIM

NAZEERA BEGUM PATHAN

Like Nephi, I was "born of goodly parents" (1 Nephi 1:1). When God sent me to this earth, He placed me in a Muslim family in the village of Parchur, in the southeast portion of India.

My father was born into a huge family. He was one of ten children. When it came time for his marriage, my uncle took him to my mother's home for the matchmaking interview. My mother was an adorable, wonderful woman, who was naturally obedient to the wishes of her parents. (In India, in times past, children obeyed their parents—and never rejected their counsel. My mother was that kind of woman.) The second my father saw my mother he fell in love with her. Though his brother wanted him to participate in a few other matchmaking interviews before he made his decision on a bride, once my father had seen my mother, he didn't want to participate in any more. He just wanted to marry her, and her alone.

After their marriage, they began their family. Times were difficult. My father struggled initially in finding work. The village they lived in had a scarcity of water, and so my mother would walk for miles each day to bring a small bucket home for our use. We lived in a small makeshift

WE LIVED IN A **SMALL MAKESHIFT SHACK,** WHICH HAD A **METAL ROOF.**

shack, which had a metal roof. During the summer, the heat in our home was nearly unbearable—both during the day and also during the long nights. When it rained, the noise inside was especially loud as the raindrops beat down upon the metal roof.

Eventually my father acquired several part-time jobs so that he could provide for our growing family. He worked as a farmer, a cashier, and also as an accountant for two different businesses. Each day he would get up at 4 a.m. so that he could farm for four hours. Then he would go to the theater, where he did accounting and worked as a cashier. He did accounting for a local garment merchant too, but he was never paid for his work there—as the man who owned the business was a friend of my fathers, and my father simply sought to help the man.

My father's various jobs provided us with the things we needed in order to live. However, they also provided the money needed for each of the children to get an education. He believed that a child's job was to study and that "education should be our life" when we were young. He wanted his children to have a good life, and he felt that education was key. Thus, though we were poor, he and my mother ensured that we children had a rather royal life. Dad worked to provide and Mom did all of the household chores so that the children could focus on getting a good education.

As Muslims, we read the Qur'an. In Islam, from a child's infancy, he or she is taught about the content of the various surahs (or chapters) of the Qur'an. Our family was no exception to this.

> **DAD** WORKED TO **PROVIDE** AND **MOM** DID ALL OF THE **HOUSEHOLD CHORES** SO THAT THE **CHILDREN** COULD FOCUS ON GETTING A **GOOD EDUCATION.**

Though I did not speak Arabic, it is a custom that each Muslim should read the entire Qur'an in Arabic at least once during their life. (Muslims traditionally hold that the Qur'an is only the Qur'an if it is in Arabic. Any translation of the Qur'an is simply "the meaning of the Qur'an," or "an interpretation of the Qur'an," but not actually the Qur'an. Arabic is the language of Allah and, thus, His words must be in Arabic, or they are not a direct quotation of what He has said.) The more one reads the Qur'an, the better one will become. Though I did not learn Arabic and, thus, couldn't read the Qur'an directly, I used to follow all of the customs of the religion, and this helped me greatly in my efforts to be a good Muslim and a good person.

In addition to reading from the Qur'an, Muslims also traditionally pray five times a day. This is called *salat* or *namaaz*. In our village, the men would go to the Mosque for *namaaz*, but the ladies would gather in one of the homes to participate in their daily prayers. My mother and my sister used to read the Qur'an at home and, on Fridays, my father and brother—along with our male cousins—would go to the mosque for prayer. Though I didn't have the chance to learn the Qur'an by reading the book, I memorized a number of its surahs (or chapters) because we recited them as part of our daily prayers. I loved when the ladies would gather together to participate in *namaaz*, even though I didn't speak Arabic and couldn't pick up all of what was being said or done.

While my parents were believing Muslims, they were not rigid with their children when it came to religious matters. They did not force us to read the Qur'an, nor did they do *namaaz* as regularly as they probably should have. As their children, they let us make many decisions regarding our personal spirituality. They gave us freedom to choose.

My mother's older sister was, in many ways, more consistent in her devotions. She taught the Qur'an to members of the community, but she also did other things to help people to submit themselves to Allah. For example, some Muslims use what is known as a *ta'wiz*—an amulet of sorts. It is a locket that has verses from the Qur'an or the *Hadith* (the sayings of Mohammed) placed inside of it. These lockets are believed to have the power to protect the wearer from evil or bad luck. My aunt and uncle would make these amulets for people—not just Muslims but Hindus and Christians too.

As we grew, my father's work responsibilities intensified. He worked very hard to provide for us. In our poverty, he did not have regular medical check-ups and did not worry about his health as he should have. In May 1997, his eyes were accidently scalded, and he lost most of his eyesight. There was no money to go to the hospital and, thus, the damage became permanent. Three days later he had what appeared

IN MAY 1997, HIS EYES WERE ACCIDENTLY SCALDED, AND HE LOST MOST OF HIS EYESIGHT.

to be a stroke and was left paralyzed from that. Here he was, a man with four dependents, unable to work. This was devastating for him and for our entire family. (We three children were young: twelve, fourteen, and sixteen years of age at the time.) My older siblings quit school in order to find work to help provide for our now destitute family. They worked hard to feed the five of us. My brother was a gifted student, but he sacrificed his desire for an education so that we would have food to eat and medicine for our father. I was too young to hold down a job. However, I did what I could to haul water and accomplish the household chores, so as to contribute what I could to our cause. Because of our father's health crisis, our family did *namaaz* as much as we could, begging God to heal him. But he continued to suffer, regularly having spasms that would sometimes last as long as a half an hour at a time. As a young girl, this scared me; I often cried, feeling helpless and hopeless.

Around this time, my sister had a Christian friend from school named Brigitte—who lived quite a distance from the church she attended. Our home was somewhere between Brigitte's hostel and the church. One Saturday she had been at church—and had been fasting. As she headed home, she realized it was too late for her to make it back to her hostel, and so she asked if she could spend the night at our home. We gladly invited her in. Around midnight, as we all slept on the floor of our shack, my father began to have one of his seizures. Our family cried as we looked on. But Brigitte told us to not cry; and she took his hand and prayed for him. Within a few minutes his seizure stopped. I was amazed, to say the least.

Not long after that, Brigitte gave us a Bible and told us to read the ninety-first Psalm whenever we were in the midst of troubles. This was the first time I had ever touched a Bible, but almost immediately, blessings began to shower down upon our family. Financial support suddenly came in from various friends—thus we were able to get our father's medications. The parents of my sister's students helped us get electricity in our home, and we were able to get a water pump so that we didn't have to haul water. We had sufficient for our living expenses and also for

> BRIGITTE **GAVE US A BIBLE** AND TOLD US TO **READ THE NINETY-FIRST PSALM** WHENEVER WE WERE IN THE **MIDST OF TROUBLES.**

my education. Though the trials brought my father a great deal of sorrow, we were very blessed during this time. And, as a consequence of those blessings, my prayers changed. Instead of praying to Allah, I began to pray to Jesus Christ.

There was a Christian church near our home. When I passed by, I would walk very slowly so that I could listen to the songs they were singing and grasp as much as I could about the

INSTEAD OF PRAYING TO **ALLAH,** I BEGAN TO PRAY TO **JESUS CHRIST.**

things they were teaching. By doing this, I also learned a little bit about how Christians pray to God—which is quite different from how Muslims pray.

Around this time, my aunt kept insisting that I come visit her at her home so that she could teach me Arabic and also the Qur'an. Though as a younger child I would have wanted to learn these things, now that I was curious about Christianity, I no longer wanted to and would gently reject her invitations by suggesting I had something else I had to do at the time.

As I grew older and my father's health did not improve, I often wanted to quit school so that I could help support my family—as my older brother and sister had done. However, my family saw in me great academic potential, and my father always felt an education was paramount, so the family encouraged me to continue my studies.

I began attending a Christian college. I loved it because I had grown to love Jesus. (Muslims believe in Jesus, but they think he was simply a prophet, not the Son of God.) Going to a Christian school gave me opportunities to learn more about Christ. We always started our classes with a hymn and prayer, and that helped me to better understand the Christian pattern for prayer.

From the time I first learned about Jesus, I loved going to church. However, I could not do so because of Islamic religious restrictions. If the religious leaders of our community became aware that I had been reading the Bible, praying to Jesus, and attending a Christian church, this could harm my family. I ran the risk of them being treated as miscreants—and being ostracized. I could not do this to my parents or siblings, particularly in light of how desperately we needed the community's help. So I secretly prayed and read the scriptures only at home.

In India, "love marriages" (those that are not arranged but are based on two people "falling in love") are not typically allowed, especially among the Muslims in my village. Girls typically would intentionally not raise their heads when in the presence of boys, so as to avoid eye contact. Consequently, I used to cover my head with a long scarf each day as I made my way to college.

Despite my efforts, a young boy named Sandeep noticed me and developed an interest in me. I was unaware, but he followed me to school most days. Eventually, he sent me a letter expressing interest in me. I was not very interested in him. (He was dark, lean, and not very attractive!) Still, his letter indicated he was a Christian and because I loved Christianity, I had great respect for anyone who was a Christian. Because I was not attracted to him, I prayed for God to remove him from my life. But the exact opposite happened. (While it may sound silly to some, I imagined myself marrying a Christian so that I could learn more about the gospel and so that I would be able to pray with my husband each day.) As Sandeep consistently expressed his love for me, I began to open my heart up to him.

Eventually I moved from my parents' home to Visakhapatnam (or Vizag), India—a port city on the Bay of Bengal—and pursued my masters of science degree. Vizag was about 250 miles from my home, so commuting was out of the question. However, this was a blessing, as I was away from those who knew me. Now I could pray and attend church openly, without fear of retribution upon my family or me. I found an Evangelical Union, where young people were taught about the gospel and learned what Christian standards for youth consisted of. I loved it! I learned so much. I participated in every event I could. I even joined the choir. My grades dipped slightly because of my focus on learning about Christ and worshipping with my friends. My parents noticed this and chastised me a bit about it, saying I was wasting my time going to church and retreats all of the time and that I should focus on my studies. While I agreed that I would pull back on some of the extra-curricular church activities, I was

> BECAUSE I WAS **NOT ATTRACTED TO HIM, I PRAYED** FOR GOD TO **REMOVE HIM FROM MY LIFE.**

bold in telling them that I would not stop attending church, and I would never convert back to Islam.

Sandeep was now my boyfriend and he and I investigated about every church we could find in Vizag. We went to Trinity Lutheran Church, the Pentecostal Church, Calvary Baptist Church, the Evangelical Church, the Kingdom Hall of Jehovah's Witnesses, and to St. Paul's Church. As we attended the various denominations, we struggled to find the peace in our hearts that we were seeking. Out of the various ones we had attended, we thought St. Paul's was probably the best, so we began going there regularly. However, I felt like the things they were teaching didn't agree with what I was reading in the Bible. One day I saw an infant being baptized via sprinkling at St. Paul's, and that struck me as wrong, so Sandeep and I decided that we didn't want to continue attending there. But we struggled to find a Church in which we felt the Spirit we were seeking. As a result, we continued to attend St. Paul's for a time, but eventually we were baptized into a Church that Sandeep's uncle ran. I thought to myself, *Finally, I have become a Christian!*—but I didn't tell my parents.

In my second year of my master's degree, I made a couple of good friends. One was Aparna Dasari, a Hindu girl who had converted to Christianity. She belonged to The Church of Jesus Christ of Latter-day Saints. (I'd never heard of it!) One day she invited Sandeep and me to attend church with her. Though we already had a Church—because she was kind, honest, loyal, and funny—we agreed to go. When we arrived, it was fast Sunday, and the members were bearing their testimonies. I found myself bothered by all of the little children who kept getting up to bear their testimonies. I found it hard to believe that small children could come to a knowledge of such things at such a young age. After sacrament meeting was over, I felt like we were rather forcefully sent to another class, and then to another. By the time church was over, I couldn't wait to leave. Sandeep and I rushed out of the building, and we determined that we would *never* go back to an LDS Church again. (Though I did not like what I experienced at Church, Aparna and I remained close friends. She married a nice returned missionary, and the two of

WE **DETERMINED** THAT WE WOULD **NEVER GO BACK** TO AN **LDS CHURCH** AGAIN.

them were incredible examples to Sandeep and me. We learned a great deal by watching the two of them.)

After this experience, we again bounced from church to church. We attended St. Paul's again and also a Baptist church. Sometimes we felt the Spirit but sometimes not. One day, Aparna invited me to church again. I was hesitant but reluctantly agreed to go. Aparna was teaching a lesson at church. As part of that lesson she showed a video of Joseph Smith's first vision. It touched my heart. That story found its way into my subconscious, and I found my heart open to the young prophet's testimony.

September 30, 2007, was a horrific day for me. Somewhere around 1 a.m., I received a phone call from my brother-in-law telling me that I needed to come home immediately. Suddenly, my uncle took the receiver and informed me that my father had died. I was stunned! My brother-in-law took the phone again and said my uncle was lying about my father's death, but that I should come home immediately. As Sandeep and I made the long trip home, the Spirit kept telling me to "be still," and it informed me that my brother-in-law had not been honest with me. The Spirit confirmed for me that my father had indeed died. But in my heart, I did not want to believe it. As we traveled, I fell asleep, and I had a dream in which I saw my father dying of a heart attack. When we finally arrived home, my family and I embraced and cried together. Our father was our strength, and now he was gone. While we were overwhelmed, at that moment I realized that Heavenly Father is the Father of us all—and He will *always* care for us, and we can *always* reach out to Him—*anytime.* The death of my earthly father gave me a strong testimony, not only of the existence of the Spirit and its ability to communicate with us but also that God gives revelation to guide and comfort His children.

GOD GIVES REVELATION TO GUIDE AND COMFORT HIS CHILDREN.

After graduation, I landed a very good job in Mumbai—more than seventeen hours from my parents' home. Family members expressed concern, as Mumbai is thought to not be a safe place for young women. However, I was not scared. I would be working for a large company, and they would watch over us. They had company housing for us to live in, and I felt certain that I would be safe.

When I arrived in Mumbai, I wondered, *How will I ever find a church to attend in this very foreign place?* I knew no Christians there and assumed that most of the Muslims and Hindus in Mumbai were not going to be able to point me to a good Christian church. For two months I literally cried and prayed to God to help me find a place to worship Him in. I had no idea where to go, but I believed that God did—and He would surely lead me to a church. I thought of the promise made in Joshua 1:9—"Be strong and of a good courage; be not afraid, neither be thou dismayed: for the Lord thy God is with thee whithersoever thou goest."

I was overwhelmed by the size of the city of Mumbai. Fortunately, the company I was working for gave the employees accommodations for the first three months so that we would have time to find a place of our own. While these lodgings were a significant distance from work, they also provided shuttles to and from work, and also buses on Sundays so that we could get to the nearest city to do our shopping. I asked one of my colleagues if he knew if there were any Christian churches nearby. He was not a Christian, but he had a friend who was, and he introduced me to his friend. The next Sunday we went to church together and, much to my surprise, it was the very Church I said I would *never* again attend: The Church of Jesus Christ of Latter-day Saints. And, to add to my disappointment, once again it happened to be fast Sunday! But I entered with my new LDS friend and worshipped alongside of him. I actually felt the Spirit and stood and bore my testimony about how I was desperate to find a Church, and God had led me to one. (I *did* believe that God had led me to the LDS Church as an answer to my prayer. I wasn't thrilled that *this* was the Church He led me to, but His will seemed more important than mine.)

The following Sunday I went to another Church that I had located during the week, but something was missing there. I didn't feel the Spirit as I had the week before. I told Sandeep about my experience and the feeling that I was having that I needed to go back to the Mormon Church. He told me, "No." He didn't want me to attend the LDS Church. I was pained by all of this. Over the next six months, the members of the LDS Church would frequently call me on Saturdays and Sundays to invite me to church, but I often would decline. I had such mixed emotions. I knew what I had felt the first time I had attended, but I also clearly remembered what I had experienced when I had watched the video of the first vision—and when I had borne my testimony in sacrament meeting. Also, I knew what I felt God wanted me to do, but I also knew what the man I loved wanted. In many ways, I was in a paradox and didn't know what to do. Because I knew I had felt the Spirit more than once in attending the Mormon Church, I also knew that I needed to go back. So I began to attend regularly. When I told my friend Aparna about how God had led me to her Church, she said, "God loves you and wants to use you for His service. Please don't leave the gospel, ever! But don't become a member except if you gain a testimony for yourself." That really touched me. Over the next year I investigated the Church and frequently discussed it with friends, and I was finally baptized—this time by proper priesthood authority—on August 9, 2009. (I did not tell my family back home of the decision I had made to join the Church.)

> "DON'T BECOME A **MEMBER** EXCEPT IF YOU **GAIN A TESTIMONY** FOR YOURSELF."

In December 2009, I had to go to Australia on a work assignment. While there I received my testimony of the Book of Mormon. I had just completed reading the *Gospel Principles* manual and, thus, picked up the Book of Mormon and began to read it. As I read, I felt the Spirit's sweet witness that what I was reading was true. I just knew! I returned to India with a testimony of that book—and with a deeper testimony of the restored gospel. I came to realize that, for me, I would learn of the truthfulness of the gospel little by little, bit by bit. I would gain a testimony of this and that, one piece at a time. I started loving the gospel and the Church more each day, and I had such a strong desire to enter the holy temple.

Over time, Sandeep's harsh feelings about the Church subsided. He too investigated it and, a year after my baptism, was baptized. Remarkably, God had softened both of our hearts toward the Church we had so fully rejected after our first encounter with it.

My family wanted me to marry Sandeep, but they knew he was a Christian and wanted him to convert to Islam before he married me. While I've always felt that the love of my family for me was unconditional, my mother did not want me marrying a Christian man. My mother felt—and rightfully so—that if the Muslim members of our community knew

I had married a Christian, it would have consequences for our family. My mother felt they might be banished. Thus, she continued to pressure Sandeep to convert to Islam because of the fears she had about how this marriage would influence the family, but also because she believed in her heart that Islam was the true religion—and that Jesus was nothing more than one of Allah's prophets. As the pressure continued, I finally had to be bold with my family and let them know that nothing they would ever say would convert us to Islam; we were converted to Christ! They felt the force and spirit of my words and, at that point, they dropped all discussion of our conversion.

In July 2013, Sandeep, our baby daughter, and I traveled to the Hong Kong temple, where Sandeep and I received our endowment and we were sealed as a family for time and all eternity. On our short trip, we not only received our own ordinances, but we also did many temple ordinances for our deceased ancestors. Those are precious days to me. The temple was our dream place, and I loved that I could look out the widow of our hotel room at night and see it. We felt the Spirit there. While within its walls, my worries about work and life seemed to melt away, and I had a peace in my heart that made me feel light and almost carefree. I was so sad the day we had to

THE TEMPLE WAS OUR DREAM PLACE.

leave Hong Kong for India, yet I thank God that we were blessed to have that experience in the temple and its accompanying joy. I am indebted to The Church of Jesus Christ of Latter-day Saints, which not only teaches us about the fullness of the gospel, but also about the central place of the family in God's plan. I thank God for the gospel that has enabled me to feel His love and compassion and has allowed me to feel His Spirit so closely and so frequently. I am ever grateful to Jesus for giving me the opportunity to truly repent and feel of the remission He offers for sin— *even my sins!* I know Christ to be a compassionate, loving, and kind being who can truly change hearts, as He has truly changed mine!

NAZEERA

A LESSON TO BE LEARNED

Satan certainly does not want *any* of God's children to embrace the restored gospel of Jesus Christ and he will do all within his power to create roadblocks to our salvation. However, President Lorenzo Snow noted that "as we improve and advance, and develop the attributes of deity within us, God will remove from our path the impediments and obstacles to our progress that are found therein."[1] Nazeera's conversion story highlights this truth. Since she could not fully learn about the gospel where she was living, like Abraham of old, the Lord simply moved her to where she could—and then placed around her individuals who had the truth. Her earnest desire to know God and exercise faith in Him made this miracle possible. But God also set up the circumstances wherein she would feel compelled to move, and whereby she would encounter the truth.

ALONZO

NOTES

1.	Lorenzo Snow, *Teachings of Lorenzo Snow*, comp. Clyde J. Williams (Salt Lake City: Bookcraft, 1984), 69.

GREEK ORTHODOX

ALONZO L. GASKILL

In the introduction to his book, *The Promised Messiah*, Elder Bruce R. McConkie wrote, "I was born with a testimony, and from my earliest days have known with absolute certainty of the truth and divinity of his great latter-day work. Doubt and uncertainty have been as foreign to me as the gibberish of alien tongues."[1] I resonate with Elder McConkie's witness—but not because I have always known that Mormonism was true. Indeed, I didn't convert to The Church of Jesus Christ of Latter-day Saints until I was an adult. However, I feel a kinship with Elder McConkie's witness because I was born with a sense of the sacred. I have always felt there was a God. I have ever felt drawn to Him. From my earliest memories, church, prayer, and ritual have been attractive to me—and a desire to connect with God in some deep, meaningful way has been my continual quest. Such things seem to be woven into my DNA. I was simply born with an innate spirituality that I cannot take credit for.

> I HAVE **ALWAYS FELT** THERE WAS A **GOD.**

By all of this, no one need suppose that I am the Mormon equivalent of a Catholic or Orthodox saint. While I consider myself deeply religious, I also have a native cheery temperament and am a man who is easily inclined to laughter. I love Heber C. Kimball's description of God's nature: "I am perfectly satisfied that my Father and my God is a cheerful, pleasant, lively, and good-natured Being. Why? Because I am cheerful, pleasant, lively, and good-natured when I have His Spirit."[2] I believe this, and I try to live it every day!

I was reared in the Greek Orthodox faith. My maternal grandparents emigrated from Greece to the United States when they were children. I have memories of attending the Orthodox Church as a young child, though I do not recall how active we were in those early years. I do, however, remember my mother teaching me when I was very young to pray (in Greek) to the Virgin Mary each night before I went to bed.

When I was about six years of age, our family moved—and the Orthodox congregation we attended built a new building. Those two factors—and perhaps others that I don't recall—caused my family to slide into semi-inactivity. We continued to attend weddings and funerals that were held at the Church, and each year during Holy Week (when Easter and the events leading up to Christ's death and resurrection are commemorated), we faithfully made our way to the Church. But regular Sunday attendees we were not for a number of years.

At some point in those early years, a faithful Sunday School teacher suggested to me that families should pray before meals. Though we had not been doing so as a family, that felt right to me. We began to have regular family prayer at dinner each night. I often offered the same short memorized prayer and then concluded by making the sign of the cross. It was a simple act, but it somehow helped me to feel closer to my Father in Heaven.

When I was around fifteen years old, I began to attend church with my maternal grandfather, who lived with us. He didn't attend every Sunday, but was more active than the rest of the family. After a month or two of sporadic attendance with him, I felt I wanted to attend weekly. And thus began my reactivation into the Greek Orthodox Church. I soon became an altar boy and didn't miss many Sundays over the next few years.

While our congregation didn't discuss much in the way of doctrine, I loved the Church. I loved its art and architecture. I

I SOON BECAME AN **ALTAR BOY** AND **DIDN'T MISS** MANY **SUNDAYS** OVER THE **NEXT FEW YEARS.**

loved the music, the incense, the candles, and the splendor of the High-Church liturgy. I felt holy when I attended, and I felt accepted by God for my efforts. The Orthodox Church teaches that it is the "true" Christian denomination—and I was very comfortable with that proclamation. Over the next four years I was very engaged and—in many ways—developed in my Christianity because of the influence of the Church in my life. I was certainly not a perfect adolescent, and I struggled with my humanity then, just as I do now. But the Orthodox Church was a profound influence for good in my life as I navigated my teenage years.

THE **ORTHODOX CHURCH** WAS A **PROFOUND INFLUENCE** FOR **GOOD** IN MY LIFE AS I NAVIGATED MY **TEENAGE YEARS.**

During high school, I knew a handful of Latter-day Saints, though they were a minority in the town in which I lived and in the school that I attended. By my sophomore year, I had become best friends with one of them. I suppose Ken and I were drawn to each other because we had similar personalities, but I was also drawn to him because of the standards I saw in him. He seemed very committed to his religion, and he was very comfortable openly living it and talking about it. (While I was a believer in my own tradition, I did not publicly manifest the same personal pride in my denomination that Ken manifested in his. That impressed me about him.)

Though the two of us spent a great deal of time together, strangely, I never felt proselyted by him. He lived his religion openly around me, but he didn't ever seem to be seeking to convince me that his Church was right or that mine was wrong. Perhaps he was hesitant to proselyte because he knew I was committed to my own faith. Or perhaps he held back because he knew I was pretty opinionated. Or quite possibly, he was reticent to push very hard owing to my occasional anti-Mormon remark. I don't really know why he didn't try harder to get me into his Church, but I do know that seeds were planted in me by simply spending time with him.

At some point, near the end of our senior year of high school, Ken invited me to attend church with him. I agreed, on the condition that he would attend the Greek Orthodox Church with me. He said he would, and so we each paid a visit to the other's worship services. Ken found the Orthodox experience a little too ritualistic and pretty "weird." I found the Mormon sacrament meeting a little too void of ritual, and—to be honest—pretty darn "boring." (To be clear, I didn't get the theology of the Saints, so the sacrament meeting talks didn't mean much to me. And I was so used to chanting, incense, candles, icons, and rituals, that the LDS sacrament meeting felt very foreign to me.) Having attended each other's services once, I think we both felt no desire to return.

> I FOUND THE **MORMON SACRAMENT MEETING** A LITTLE TOO **VOID OF RITUAL,** AND—TO BE HONEST—PRETTY DARN **"BORING."**

At the conclusion of that year, we each graduated from high school. Ken anticipated serving a mission, and I was off to the university. Still active in the Orthodox faith, I was dismayed to discover that the town in which I would be attending college—which was several hours from my home—had no Orthodox Church. What was I to do? All but one of my roommates were Roman Catholic, so I decided I would just attend Church with them. I tried doing so for a while, but I simply didn't feel at home there. Some spiritual piece was missing for me and, so, I knew I needed to try something else. I was taking a number of theology courses at the time and, consequently, I determined that I would just go to a different religion each week until I could attend the Greek Orthodox Church (on my occasional trips home). I visited the mosque, the synagogue, meetings of the Campus Crusade for Christ, etc. If I could find it, I would attend it. At this point, I was visiting these various faiths mostly out of intellectual curiosity. I certainly wasn't looking to convert to anything and was quite happy as an Eastern Orthodox Christian. But, since my circumstances made attendance at my church of choice impossible, the stimulating encounter of learning about what others believe and do would have to suffice.

One Monday afternoon I saw an LDS Institute of Religion building on campus. I recall thinking, *Hey, that's Ken's Church. I should just check that out one more time too.* I approached the door but found it locked. As I turned and began to walk away, a young woman came to the door and invited me in. We chatted for twenty minutes or so, and then Erin—the young women whom I had been speaking with—asked me if I had plans that evening. She indicated that the students who attended that ward held a group Family Home Evening each Monday night, and I was welcome to attend. I accepted the invitation and joined them for board games and ice cream. (Suspiciously, I won pretty much everything we played that evening. I'm not bad at games, but I'm pretty sure I'm not that good either. I suspect this was some kind of missionary technique, and it didn't go unnoticed.) At the conclusion of our evening together, Newell, one of the attendees, asked me what I was doing Wednesday. I indicated that I wasn't sure. He said they had a service project they were doing, and he wondered if I could help out. I agreed to, and met up with them on Wednesday. After the midweek service project, another member of the group asked what I was doing on Sunday. I indicated that I was Greek Orthodox, but that—for the time being—I was just attending various religions each week. He invited me to attend with them, and so I agreed that I would that Sunday. Perhaps because it was a singles ward—or perhaps because I was in a different place theologically than I had been a year or two earlier—the meeting didn't seem so boring this time. I quite enjoyed my experience.

Well, before long it seemed I was in a Monday/Wednesday/Sunday cycle with my newfound Latter-day Saint friends. I enjoyed being with them, but what I was really enjoying was talking to the missionaries. I would not in any way classify myself as having been anti-Mormon, but I certainly had some wrongheaded ideas about the LDS Church—its doctrines, practices, and history—and I wasn't uncomfortable pointing those out. Consequently, the missionaries and I really didn't ever get to the standard discussions. We spent most of our time talking about some of my misconceptions. I would ask my questions and they would do their best to answer them. If they were unable, they would traditionally promise that, if I would allow them to come back in a couple of days, they would have an answer for me—and they always did!

Though I was spending an increasing amount of time with the Latter-day Saints, I was still visiting other religions also. On one occasion I was in a Campus Crusade for Christ meeting, and a large group of us were sitting around talking about our favorite movies. (At that time mine happened to be a movie about Thomas Becket, the twelfth-century Archbishop of Canterbury. I know, weird! Huh?!) At some point in the conversation, I made a joke about the Mormons. The CCC folks loved it. There was sustained laughter; and yet I had the strangest experience. Immediately after I told the joke, I was enveloped by a tangible darkness. While I could not understand the full meaning of the experience at the time, I felt as though God was somehow unhappy with me for what I had just done. I tried to play it off by pretending to laugh with the rest of the group, but I knew I had crossed a line—and the physical darkness I felt shocked me. It left an indelible impression on me that I have never forgotten. This was the first time I had felt the Holy Ghost in direct relation to the LDS Church. And, so far as I could recall, it was also the first time I recognized feeling the withdrawal of the Spirit because of something unkind I had said about a people I had actually grown quite fond of.

Shortly thereafter I had a second experience with the Spirit, which also struck me—but again, as a non-Mormon, I struggled to fully understand it at the time. When various friends became aware that I was talking with the LDS missionaries, I began to receive anti-Mormon tracts and books from concerned Christians. When I read those tracts, or when I talked to those who were seeking to "save me from the Mormons"—and from what appeared to be sure damnation—I felt dark, confused, frustrated, and more. However, when I was talking with the missionaries, attending the LDS Church, reading the Bible or Book of Mormon, I felt uplifted, at peace, happy, and so on. Now, in retrospect, it seems quite obvious what the message was: "That which is of God is light" and, when we embrace and follow that light, it "groweth brighter and brighter until the perfect day" (D&C 50:24). Again, having not been taught (as a Greek Orthodox Christian) about the workings of the Holy Spirit, I didn't realize at the time what God was telling me but, in hindsight, this all seems so obvious.

Well, after several months of talking with the missionaries and attending the LDS Church and various activities, I had an experience that was pivotal in my process of conversion. I was at the institute building (where we held our church meetings), and the elders quorum president called me over and asked, rather point-blank, "Alonzo, when are you getting baptized?" I was a bit taken aback by his question, but I

"ALONZO, **WHEN ARE YOU GETTING BAPTIZED?"**

replied, "Well, if I knew it was true, I would probably get baptized. But I *don't* know that it is true, so I'm *not* getting baptized unless I know that."

He asked what I was doing to find out if it was true. I indicated that I had read parts of the Book of Mormon and I had prayed several times about the Church but simply felt that I had not received an answer. So I was uncomfortable moving forward. (*I really had* prayed many times about the Church and had felt that no answer had come. But, I must admit that the content of my prayers up to that point had basically been, "God, I'm pretty certain there is no way that this could be true. However, if I'm wrong, please let me know." And then nothing but silence would come. Obviously I wasn't really open to an answer from the Spirit until my conversation with this young man.) The elders quorum president then asked me, "Do you read the Book of Mormon every day?" I informed him that

"DO YOU **READ THE BOOK OF MORMON** EVERY DAY?"

I had a heavy course load and read the Bible every day, but I did not have time to read both *every day*, and I wasn't going to stop reading the Bible so that I could read the Book of Mormon instead. His response to me, as near as I can remember it, was simply this: "Well then, I guess you don't have time to find out if it's true. Why don't you get out of here and come back when you're really sincere about finding out?" I was absolutely floored. As I walked out of the building and made my way back to my dorm, I remember milling his words over in my mind, disappointed in his seeming harshness and somewhat saddened that a rather joyful stage of my life had come to an end. However, as I neared my residence, I was struck for the first time with the sense that he was right: *If this is true, I really* do *need to know that. And if it is false, I need to know that also—so that I can move on with my life. Indeed, if it is false*, I thought, *then I'm wasting my time and theirs*. Thus, while this young man's boldness might seem like a poor approach to missionary work, I believe he was inspired in what he said that day—and in how he said it, as it was the very thing I needed to hear to get me to pray with sincerity of heart. It was the thing that awoke me to my situation and the sacred journey I had been taking for the last few months. His words made me aware of the fact that I really *could* entertain the possibility that Mormonism could be true.

When I arrived at my dorm, I went into my bedroom, locked the door, knelt down next to my bed, and offered up one more prayer regarding the Church, the Book of Mormon, and everything else I had studied over the course of the past few months. And though I had prayed about this before, this time I really felt the importance of getting an answer; I felt a need to be willing to let God tell me—rather than *me* telling *Him*—if the Church was true.

As I explained to my Father in Heaven what I was feeling, what I understood about the doctrines of the LDS Church, I begged, "If this is true, I need you to give me something empirical so that I will really *know*, because it will absolutely devastate my parents if I leave the Orthodox Church to become a Mormon." As I pled, and then awaited my answer, I heard with clarity these words, "Dispute not because ye see not, for ye receive no witness until after the trial of your faith" (Ether 12:6). And then the thought passed through my mind, *Alonzo, you already know it's true. I cannot give you anything more until you act on what you know.* I did not realize at the time that the answer to my prayer had come in the form of words from the Book of Mormon. (Perhaps at some point I had read those words, though I do not recall doing so prior to that prayer.) Unexpectedly, my answer had come and in a way that was significant enough that I would not equivocate. I got off my knees, called my friend Ken, and asked, "How does one get baptized in the Mormon Church?"

On November 25, 1984, I joined The Church of Jesus Christ of Latter-day Saints. A week later I was ordained a priest in the Aaronic Priesthood. Less than eight months later I was ordained an elder. And less than one year after my baptism I received a mission call to England. The blessings that have been mine because of my conversion to the restored gospel are too numerous and too profoundly spiritual to describe here. But suffice it to say, every facet of my life has been influenced by the answer that came to my prayer that day: my lifestyle, the mate I chose, the education and employment I pursued, the number of children I have, even how I spend my leisure time.

THE **BLESSINGS** THAT HAVE BEEN MINE **BECAUSE OF MY CONVERSION TO THE RESTORED GOSPEL** ARE TOO **NUMEROUS** AND TOO **PROFOUNDLY SPIRITUAL** TO DESCRIBE HERE.

With all of the blessings that came to me via my conversion, it also brought some significant trials. For the better part of two decades, my relationship with my parents was greatly strained because of my membership in the Church. I don't blame them for this. I was fairly young when I converted, and I really didn't know how to deal with their discontent over my newfound faith. In addition, readily available anti-Mormon literature—though consistently inaccurate—painted a picture of Mormon theology, history, and practice that made my parents very concerned about my decision. Consequently, the relationship was harmed—and I sincerely regret that I did not handle things better.

Like so many Latter-day Saints, my conversion didn't end at baptism, or when I was ordained, or when I received my endowment, or on my mission. Conversion, if it is to have the long-lasting effect God desires it to, must be a lifelong pursuit. And, thus, I turn now to one additional element of my journey.

As silly as it will sound to some, prior to my mission, my intended career path was mortuary science. Yes, I wanted to be an undertaker! As I've looked back on what drew me to such a career, I think a number of factors played a significant role. Our Orthodox congregation was older and, consequently, funerals were frequent. My mother and I regularly attended them together. I didn't understand, doctrinally speaking, what happened to one after he or she passes from this mortal existence—but I always sensed that something sacred was taking place at the funerals I attended. For me, death was a spiritual rite of passage, and that brought feelings to my soul when I attended a funeral that I didn't feel in other settings. I wanted that spiritual feeling consistently in my life, and so mortuary science seemed to be the best way to nurture that.

PRIOR TO MY MISSION, MY INTENDED CAREER PATH WAS MORTUARY SCIENCE.

Spatial constraints won't allow me to go into the details here, but, needless to say, I didn't become an undertaker. Rather, I had an experience on my mission that ultimately sent me down an entirely different career path. By the time I had arrived back in the United States, I had determined that I wanted to teach religion for a living. I pursued a bachelor's degree in philosophy and then earned my master's and doctorate degrees in theology and biblical studies (at Catholic and Protestant graduate schools).

Upon enrolling in graduate school, I fully expected to have my beliefs called into question; I expected to discover things that would challenge my faith—particularly since I was studying religion at non-LDS schools. Yet, I can honestly say that the exact opposite happened to me. Oh, there were certainly things taught that I did not agree with. But, generally speaking, instead of discovering things that provoked doubts about my beliefs and my conversion, time and again my faith was confirmed through my academic pursuits. In the Doctrine and Covenants the Lord commands us to "seek learning, even by study and also by faith" (D&C 88:118; See also D&C 109:7, 14). My testimony of The Church of Jesus Christ of Latter-day Saints has really come through following that commission. I have faith in the restored gospel and its teachings, and that faith has come, in part, through scripture study, prayer, and personal revelation to my heart and mind. But I also have a belief in Mormonism based on an analytical, academic investigation of it. I'm as convinced intellectually of its claims as I am spiritually converted to its teachings. Finally, for me, Mormonism simply works—and because of that, I believe it! When I live it to the best of my ability, I feel the Lord's Spirit active in my life, guiding and directing me. When I live it, I have peace—even amid life's difficulties. When I am faithful to what I believe and know in my heart, I am happier, and I am kinder to those whom the Lord places in my path.

For me, the goodness of God has been manifest in my life in so many ways—but I count as one of my greatest blessings God's choice to grab me by the scruff of the neck, pick me up off the path I was on, and place me in The Church of Jesus Christ of Latter-

> WHEN I THINK OF HOW **GOOD** AND **GRACIOUS** THE **LORD HAS BEEN** TO ME, I AM AT A **LOSS FOR WORDS.**

day Saints. That grand and divinely-directed rerouting has made all the difference in my life. And when I think of how good and gracious the Lord has been to me, I am at a loss for words. And so, I close by offering the testimony of William Grimshaw, of England, who—in the eighteenth century—penned so well what I feel in my heart: "When I die, I shall then have my greatest grief and my greatest joy. My greatest grief, that I have done so little for Jesus; my greatest joy, that Jesus has done so much for me."[3]

ALONZO

A LESSON TO BE LEARNED

Over the years, when I have shared my conversion story with others, I've noticed that people are often aghast at what the elders quorum president said to me that day. Indeed, most think it was an incredibly inappropriate thing to say, something that ran the risk of pushing me away from the Church, rather than bringing me into it. In ways, I suppose they're right. But ultimately, what that young man said to me that day was the very thing I needed to hear; it was the very thing that enabled me to change my attitude, pray with sincerity and faith, and gain a witness of the restored gospel of Jesus Christ.

The Lord has counseled, "Speak the thoughts that I shall put into your hearts. . . . For it shall be given you in the very hour, yea, in the very moment, what ye shall say" (D&C 100:5–6). In a similar vein, Jesus also taught, "It shall be given you in that same hour what ye shall speak. For it is not ye that speak, but the Spirit of your Father which speaketh in you" (Matthew 10:19–20). If we ensure that we speak under the influence of the Spirit, God will grant us the gift of tongues to say the very thing those seeking truth need to hear. I thank God for a man who spoke under the influence of the Spirit that day, for it changed my life.

ALONZO

NOTES

1. Bruce R. McConkie, *The Promised Messiah: The First Coming of Christ* (Salt Lake City: Deseret Book, 1978), xvii.
2. Heber C. Kimball, in *Journal of Discourses*, 4:222.
3. William Grimshaw, *Memoirs of the Life of the Late Rev. William Grimshaw*, comp. John Newton (London: W. Baynes and Son, 1825), 141–42.

RE-CONVERSION

KEVIN WILSON

Everything is a story, and my life is no exception to that. It would have been nice if I could have learned the lessons I've learned without experiencing and causing so much pain, but what matters is that I learned them—and the lessons have been absolutely life-changing.

I grew up in the Church. I was baptized at eight years old, ordained a deacon at twelve, and then a teacher at fourteen. Unfortunately, my involvement in the Church in my Aaronic Priesthood years was a bit like wearing gym shoes to gym class—it's just what you do. It's what everyone does! Growing up in small-town Springville, Utah, I went to church because that's just what you do. But I didn't see the Church as a gift in those early years. Perhaps most kids don't.

I WENT TO CHURCH BECAUSE THAT'S JUST WHAT YOU DO.

As a kid, it seemed like we didn't have much in the way of temporal stuff. There were six kids, and I suppose that required that my parents' financial resources be spread a bit thin. So if I wanted something, I had to figure out a way to get it. Around the time I was fourteen, I landed a decent job, and I worked hard. I made good money for a teenager and used what I earned to buy whatever I wanted. I pretty quickly developed an entitlement mentality. I began to think, if I want it, I deserve it, and if I don't want to, I don't have to. (I didn't realize at the time how much I was going to suffer because of this jaded view of life.)

> I BEGAN TO THINK, **IF I WANT IT, I DESERVE IT,** AND **IF I DON'T WANT TO, I DON'T HAVE TO.**

Because I was working six days a week, I decided I didn't really want to spend my one day off at church, so I would pretend to sleep in on Sunday mornings. When my parents would try to wake me, I would just act as though I was still asleep. I simply refused to get up for church. My folks pushed pretty hard initially. However, they finally decided that riding me wasn't helping, so they backed off.

My freshman year of high school I made the varsity baseball team. I was a left-handed pitcher who, by the time I was seventeen, could throw a ninety-mile-an-hour pitch. As a sophomore, I was invited by the Kansas City Royals to try out for their team, and as junior I was courted by the Cincinnati Reds. So I started to think I was a pretty big deal and, consequently, I kind of cut loose and did whatever I wanted. (Because I was important to the team, my coaches made sure I passed all of my classes.) I really thought I was king of the world.

My junior year our team won state. The Reds were calling like crazy, and I had an offer to play college ball also. Then, the summer before my senior year, I threw my arm out. I had surgery but ended up getting a staph infection as a result of the operation. Instead of getting better before the baseball season, I got worse—and couldn't even walk for a time because the infection had found its way to my hip. I was hospitalized for about five or six weeks, and I missed tryouts for the upcoming season. In a matter of a month and a half I went from being king of the world to missing

> IN A MATTER OF **A MONTH AND A HALF** I WENT FROM BEING **KING OF THE WORLD** TO **MISSING TRYOUTS** AND BEING **DROPPED FROM THE TEAM.**

tryouts and being dropped from the team. My world suddenly collapsed.

132

When I was released from the hospital and sent home to recuperate, the doctors provided me with a significant amount of pain medication. Those took care of the physical pain but also seemed to help with the emotional pain of losing my promising baseball career. My sense of personal value was heavily wrapped up in my gifts as a baseball player and, once that was gone, so was my sense of worth.

The doctors eventually told me I was well enough to be off the pain meds, but I didn't emotionally feel ready to be done with them. When my physician wouldn't give me any more, I found friends who would. Over time, I went from prescription pain meds to cocaine and heroin and ultimately found myself in legal trouble. But again, because of my stardom as a baseball player, various people pulled strings to mitigate the consequences of my bad choices. Of course, this only reinforced the feeling I had that I could do whatever I wanted without consequences. I felt invincible.

> OVER TIME, I WENT FROM **PRESCRIPTION PAIN MEDS** TO **COCAINE AND HEROIN** AND ULTIMATELY FOUND MYSELF IN **LEGAL TROUBLE.**

In the ensuing months and years, my addictions increased, as did my brushes with the law. I had lost all control of my life. My addictions were now in the driver's seat. At the age of eighteen, I had my first heart attack; I was dead for about two minutes. When I was resuscitated, I remember feeling the weight of coming back to my awful life, and it felt incredibly heavy. I remember thinking that because of my drug dependency, dying from a drug overdose was more peaceful to me than being alive.

Not long after my heart attack, I entered a rehab and got "clean," and I remained drug-free for about eighteen months. But I came home one day and found my little brother getting high with one of his friends, and instead of warning them about the dangers of substance abuse, I joined them. I was immediately back into the throws of my addiction, and before long, my brother and I were in legal trouble. (We had broken into a business and stolen sixteen thousand dollars.)

Knowing I was in serious trouble, I fled the state of Utah, initially heading for California, but eventually landing in Tijuana, Mexico—where

I took a job smuggling people across the border. (While I didn't know it at the time, shortly before I left for Mexico, my mother's brothers gave her a powerful priesthood blessing in which she was promised that "legions of angels" would be with me to keep me safe. On so many occasions, the blessing was fulfilled.)

In Tijuana, I was paid eight hundred dollars for each car I drove across the border. This newfound income served to feed my drug habit. It got worse and worse, and I eventually found myself in the federal felony holding tank in San Diego, where I was incarcerated for seventy-two days. During that time, I went through intensely painful drug withdrawals. From California, I was sent to Utah, where I spent the next eight months in jail for crimes I had committed there.

> I WAS PAID **EIGHT HUNDRED DOLLARS** FOR **EACH CAR** I DROVE ACROSS THE **BORDER.**

When I was eventually released, my parents kept telling me, "You need to get back to Church." But because of all of the horrible things I had done wrong, I kept thinking, *I can't! I can't! There is no possible way I can be forgiven for this. This will all have to be sorted out in the next life.*

Miraculously, for the next four years I was largely drug free. I still drank and chewed tobacco, but the hard drugs were not part of my life. I became a workaholic as a means of keeping myself out of trouble—and I excelled at my job. However, I was not in a healthy place emotionally. I had not taken care of my past and so, when I sought out relationships, I looked for women with similar issues as mine—because I knew that they would accept me. Of course, that's a recipe for disaster in a marriage. I married a gal who had her own issues and we had two children together. But the relationship was not a good one. The only good things that came from our marriage were my two boys. Indeed, having kids was the first happy thing that had happened to me since my days of playing baseball.

> HAVING **KIDS** WAS THE **FIRST HAPPY THING** THAT HAD HAPPENED TO ME **SINCE** MY DAYS OF **PLAYING BASEBALL.**

In time, I hurt my back and the doctor put me on painkillers. I kept thinking while I was at the doctor's office, *You need to tell him you're an addict.* But I didn't—and I quickly got hooked again. Rather than getting the help I needed for my various issues, I simply threw myself into my work, and I worked like crazy. I was seldom home, and I never helped out with the kids. My wife and I were both battling some pretty serious "monsters," and our kids were largely neglected. The marriage ultimately ended in a divorce.

At one point (prior to our divorce) my sons' mom and I were arrested for check fraud. We were driving with the boys in the pickup truck when the police pulled us over. I remember both of us being handcuffed and shoved into patrol cars as my two boys sat in the truck screaming. There was an absolute look of terror on their faces. They felt such fear, and their mother and I were the cause of it. That image has haunted me for years. (When I finally began my recovery, I was able to use that indelibly ingrained memory as a reminder when things got hard.)

My parents took the kids while the Division of Child and Family Services (DCFS) started the paperwork to put my boys in "the system." I got out of jail and went to my parents' home—where my kids were staying. DCFS was there, so I began to do my "song and dance" so as to convince them that they should give me my kids back. But it didn't work this time. The caseworker said to me, "You need to leave. You're a threat to your children." Though I was absolutely furious, in my heart of hearts I knew what he said was

"YOU NEED TO **LEAVE.** YOU'RE A **THREAT TO YOUR CHILDREN.**"

the truth. I asked him, "Where am I supposed to go?" He said, "I don't care! But you can't be around your kids because you pose a danger to them."

You would think this would be sufficient to get me to clean up my act, but it wasn't. I continued to use. I often missed my scheduled drug tests—or came to them while I had drugs in my system. At one of my court dates I was told by DCFS, "If you don't clean yourself up, we're going to terminate your parental rights." I was so overwhelmed, I went and procured as many drugs as I could and then begged God to let me die of an overdose. As I drove home, I told myself, "If I love those kids more than myself, tomorrow morning I will go down to the court house and I will sign away my parental rights." I knew I needed to love them enough to give them a better life. But the guilt of knowing that I would have to watch them be raised by someone else because I loved drugs more than them just destroyed me. I went home, took some drugs, and passed out. At around 12:30 a.m., the joint criminal apprehension team kicked my door in. (There was a warrant out for my arrest, though I was unaware of it at the time.) They threw me in jail and I came to grips with the fact that the worst thing in my children's lives was *me*.

THE WORST THING IN MY CHILDREN'S LIVES WAS ME.

Once again, while incarcerated, I began to go through drug withdrawals. In the midst of suffering through that, one of the guards asked if anyone wanted to go to the LDS 12 Steps recovery meeting that day. I decided to go, just to get my mind off of the pain of the withdrawals. As I sat there listening, I felt so defeated. The next day I went back, and one of the senior missionaries—a guy named Merlin—played for us a tape recording of a little girl singing "I Am a Child of God." It hit me in an unexpected way. I began to sob uncontrollably. I had come to the conclusion that I was of no value—not even to my children—and here was this song saying I was of significant worth. At the end of the song, Merlin said, "How many of you have kids?" I raised my hand. He said, "Do you remember when they were born?" I said, "I do! They were the only two good days of my life in the last eight years." He said, "Do you remember the love you felt for them the day they were born?" And I said, "Yes! It was so thick you could cut it with a knife." Merlin said, "That is just a *tiny* glimpse of how much Heavenly Father loves *you*." At that point I began to bawl again. I had this inner conflict: what I believed about myself and what this missionary was telling me God felt about me. For the next few days I prayed and cried and poured my soul out to God. "I'm not asking you to fix this," I remember saying. "I'll do what work I can to repair what I've done. But I just need to know that you're in my corner. I need to know that that song is right—that I *am* a child of God. If what Merlin said

"I JUST NEED TO KNOW THAT YOU'RE IN MY CORNER."

about love is true, and if that song is true—and if you're in my corner— then I can do this. I don't know how, but I will do this."

Unexpectedly, two days later I was released from jail. I was terrified to leave. My dad came and got me, gave me forty dollars and his pickup truck, and then said to me, "Son, I love you to pieces, but you cannot be here. You're a threat to your children, and I will protect them from you at all costs." That was a hard thing to hear. I didn't know what I was going to do, but I left. And the thought that came to mind was simply this, *The only place I've felt safe was in the addiction recovery meetings.* So I immediately started looking for a meeting. I found an LDS 12 Steps gathering in Provo, so I went directly there. Part of me didn't want to be there, but I stayed and that day I didn't have to fight the "monster." I was feeling the Spirit, and I felt better. It didn't fix anything, but—for one day—I didn't have to fight the "monster." I thought to myself, *I'm doing this every day!* I had no intention of doing the formal steps and the workbook, but I was committed to going to go to the meetings every day so I wouldn't have to fight the "monster" anymore. I went back the next day and the next. And I was clean. DCFS was surprised but happy with my progress. My one-hour supervised visits with my boys were hard for me, however. I couldn't stand seeing the hurt on their faces—hurt I had caused.

I COULDN'T STAND SEEING THE HURT ON THEIR FACES—HURT I HAD CAUSED.

I continued to go to my 12 Steps meetings regularly. In a way, I was still in the same cycle of dependence as in the past but now it was meetings, not drugs. So I actually started doing the program properly—working my way through each of the steps. And I was getting better. I continued to attend the meetings *every single day!* I was "chasing the Spirit" every single day. I didn't know it was the Spirit at the time, but it was—and I *had to* chase it. I needed it constantly so that I would have the strength to fight my "monster."

After about six months, I had to go back to see the judge over an unresolved felony check charge. My lawyer told me, "You're going to prison. With your list of crimes and your background, there's no chance that you're getting off on this one. You're going to prison." I was resigned to the fact that I might actually go to prison, and if that's what I had to do, I would do it. I knew that, for the first time in my life, I trusted God. So if going to jail was what was best for me, then I was comfortable with that decision. I believed that God had my best interest in mind. (This really was a turning point for me.) Amazingly, I was given "one more chance!"

I ended up adopting a motto in my life: "If I don't want to, I need to"—because, when I'm chasing what *I* want, it's usually destructive. So I decided, if I don't want to do something, then I *need* to do it. I knew that would help to reprogram me. I didn't want to go to church, and I certainly didn't want to go to the ward my boys went to—because that was my parents' ward. I knew everyone in that ward, and they all knew why my boys were there with my parents instead of with me. Since I didn't want to go there, I knew I needed to—and I decided that I would. Walking into that building was the hardest thing I had done—harder than standing before a judge that could send me to prison. But I kept telling myself, "I need this. I need this." So my visits with my boys for the next six weeks consisted of going to church with them at my folk's ward.

I began attending church every week again. I hadn't done so since I was fourteen years old. I had a great bishop—Bishop Holden. And the principles I was learning and applying were working. They were changing my life. Whenever I had struggles, where I couldn't keep my head right, I would pray. I would tell God, "I can't do this. I need you to help me." And He always would. I would make it through my temptations or struggles. My boys could see the changes in my life, and things were going well.

I started meeting with the bishop regularly, so that I could work my way through the repentance process. Through those meetings I developed a close relationship with Bishop Holden—and he became my best friend. However, in the midst of the repentance process, the bishop informed me that he was moving and, thus, would no longer be my bishop. I remember thinking to myself, *Great! I'm going to have to start this whole process over again.* And so I met with the new bishop—Bishop Dickenson—and it was the most amazing thing. I walked in there, I sat down, and there

IT'S **NOT THE** BISHOP THAT IS MY BEST FRIEND; IT'S THE **SAVIOR.**

across the desk from me sat my best friend. He and I started right where I had left off with Bishop Holden. And it struck me: it's not the bishop that is my best friend; it's the Savior. I've been sitting here having conversations with the Savior—through the bishop's mantle of authority. The love that I felt, and the inspired counsel that I received, wasn't from Bishop Holden or Bishop Dickenson, it was the Savior. He was, *and is*, my best friend! I had been having a one-on-one with Christ through the mantle of the bishop. I was overwhelmed as I began to realize this. This realization convinced me that men were not running the Church; it was being run, through inspiration, by God. And if you were to take away the mantles of authority that bishops, stake presidents, or prophets have, it would all collapse in no time at all.

The message of my conversion is really found in Doctrine and Covenants 18:10—"The worth of souls is great in the sight of God." Satan wants me and you to underestimate our value. Yet, our ability to become as God makes our value limitless. However, our willingness to embrace that capacity changes everything. If we refuse to embrace that truth, Satan wins! But, if we fully accept it, we can become as God, and our value becomes limitless.

There were a couple of things that enabled the testimony that I had had since I was a little child to become the conversion I needed as an adult. First, the day I gave up my will, starting with the moment I stood before the judge facing prison time. When I realized that I could be okay being locked away if that was God's will—as I was convinced God had what was best for me in mind—that's when I found the strength to turn other parts of my life over to Him. The second element of conversion was when I realized that the bishop's mantle was really Christ's mantle resting upon a mortal representative of Him. That enabled me to *know* the Church was indeed run by God. Those two experiences enabled me to transition from being a guy who believed the Church was probably true, to a man

"LIVING MY FAITH IS THE BEST THING I HAVE EVER DONE WRONG!"

who was committed to living it to the best of his ability—including being willing to "give away all my sins to know" Him (Alma 22:18). Of course, I'm not perfect. I tell people, "Living my faith is the best thing I have ever done wrong!" In other words, I struggle to do it right, but I do it! And I keep chasing the Spirit!

Finally, I have to emphasize that the thing that saved me was coming to an understanding that God loves me, that *I am* a child of God! That brought about my willingness to try to change. It wasn't the chastisement—and I received plenty of that during my battle with addiction. It wasn't an awareness that I was hurting others that changed me. And it wasn't the guilt; you can't guilt someone into changing. It was knowing that God loves me that made the difference in my life. My life is a testimony to the power of the Savior's love.

KEVIN

A LESSON TO BE LEARNED

There seem to have been a couple of important factors in Kevin's conversion. First, he felt the Spirit tell him that, regardless of what he thought in his head, God loves His children—and *always* will. For someone who was so filled with self-loathing, what a joyous realization that had to have been. If you and I can get to the point that we know and believe that sacred truth—and I mean *really believe* it—then God can heal *anything* wrong in our lives.

A second lesson from Kevin's conversion is the truth that God speaks inspired words through His servants. The bishop has a mantle; the stake president has a mantle; missionaries have mantles; and the Lord's prophets have mantles. When we come to that realization, we'll then know that there is so much help to be had whenever we struggle.

Finally, I was touched by Kevin's comment that he continually "chased the Spirit." The Holy Ghost is absolutely foundational to any true conversion. It is necessary to get a testimony, and it is necessary to retain one. You and I must unceasingly "chase the Spirit" if we hope to have the strength to endure a sin-filled and trial-laden world. But if, like Kevin, we "chase" it every day, our testimonies will burn bright and our salvation will be assured.

ALONZO

REORGANIZED CHURCH OF JESUS CHRIST OF LATTER DAY SAINTS

DENNIS CATO

I was born a fourth generation member of the Reorganized Church of Jesus Christ of Latter Day Saints (now called Community of Christ), sometimes referred to as the RLDS Church. My great-grandfather served as a missionary for the Reorganized Church. My grandfather served on the standing high council (which advises the First Presidency and Presiding Bishopric), and my father was a pastor over a local RLDS congregation.

In the late 1960s and throughout the ensuing decades, the RLDS Church began to experience significant shifts in its doctrine and practice. What once had been a denomination of the Restoration, suddenly began to take on the appearance of a mainline Protestant church. Many who had been faithful, believing members, suddenly found themselves somewhat dismayed as the leadership of their Church began to reject many traditional teachings of the restored gospel. Joseph Smith and the Book of Mormon would both ultimately become casualties of this shift in emphasis. And many of the faithful would feel that they had had the rug pulled out from underneath them as the things they had always been taught by the leadership of the Church were now being discounted, dismissed, and discarded.

I was one of the dismayed. Having developed in my youth a strong testimony of the Restoration and the divine call of the Prophet Joseph Smith, I was bewildered as the Church that I loved and believed in began to call into question things I had always known to be true. Leaders of the RLDS Church began to ask questions, such as: "How do we explain Joseph Smith's first vision?" "Where in mainstream Christianity does the Restoration fit?" and "How do we stay relevant as a Church when our history and theology seems so puritanical?"

It became apparent to me that my Church was stepping away from its restoration focus and from the direction established by previous prophets. The Church I had grown up in and loved suddenly seemed more concerned with appearing mainstream than with defending the doctrines of the Restoration.

For my wife and me, the breaking point came during the 1984 biennial general conference of the RLDS Church. During that meeting a document was presented to the conference by Wallace B. Smith, who was at that time President of the Church. In this document—which would become section 156 of the RLDS Doctrine and Covenants—Wallace B. Smith declared what he deemed the will of the Lord, in these words: "It is my will that my priesthood be made up of those who have an abiding faith and desire to serve me with all their hearts, in humility and with great devotion. . . . Therefore, do not wonder that some women of the church are being called to priesthood responsibilities. This is in harmony with my will" (RLDS D&C 156:8a & 9c).

> "DO NOT WONDER THAT SOME WOMEN OF THE CHURCH ARE BEING CALLED TO PRIESTHOOD RESPONSIBILITIES."

With this announcement, my wife and I determined that we could no longer remain members of the RLDS Church. How could we support an organization that seemed to be straying from the course charted by the Prophet Joseph?

We were not alone in our concerns. During this era there were a significant number of members of the RLDS Church who had become disaffected and who sought to organize into groups that could meet together and continue teaching the doctrines originally espoused by the Reorganization. The folks who organized or joined these various groups felt they could no longer support the leadership and teachings of the Church. The title "remnant groups" or "restoration groups" became the accepted way to refer to these splinter organizations. Several started their own Churches (The Remnant Church, the Joint Conference of Restoration Branches, etc.), but many just wanted to return to the past teachings of the RLDS Church, as these were a source of comfort and peace to them.

As my wife and I thought about our future, a determination was made that we should try to meet in one of these groups. So we sought out individuals and families who believed as we did regarding the Restoration, Joseph Smith, and the Book of Mormon. Of course, we realized that we had no authority to start a new Church, but we desperately desired to meet with people of like faith—both for fellowship, and also to keep the truths of the Restoration alive.

In an effort to organize, I began to seek out my closest friends from the RLDS Church. There were five brethren whom I had served with in the Priesthood—each of whom was struggling with the direction of the Church. A meeting was scheduled, and we came together to discuss what the most appropriate approach to our dilemma was. As we prayerfully put our heads together, a consensus was reached and plans were made to begin holding regular worship services together. At this point, all decisions were made by counsel. We pooled our financial resources and rented an elementary school gym that was available on Sundays. The first Sabbath we met together, sixty-five people attended our meetings. Within a few weeks we had over a hundred people in attendance at our weekly meetings. We were quickly outgrowing the school facility, and so we had to move to a larger building. (This was a great problem to have.) In three years we had three hundred people regularly attending our meetings.

WE DESPERATELY DESIRED TO MEET WITH PEOPLE OF LIKE FAITH.

It was at this point we began looking for a building of our own. There was a church, of another denomination, that was for sale just off the square in Independence, Missouri. The original counsel of six Elders looked at options. How could we do this? What were the legal options to ownership? We determined to develop a "charitable trust." No one person would have ownership. If the group failed, the building would be sold and the funds given to a local charity.

We presented our idea to the membership. Everyone was in favor of moving forward, and so an offer was made on the property and we were able to purchase it. Our growing congregation now had a permanent home. We were thrilled. As a "church family," we worked side by side, painting our new "home," planting flowers and shrubs, and beautifying our new place of worship. There was a sense of pride in what we had accomplished; not only that we had acquired our own building to meet in but also in the success of our group. We had stepped away from the general Church, and yet we were thriving. And though we felt the Church was leaving the message of the Restoration and Reorganization, we were keeping it alive among ourselves. We couldn't help but feel good about that.

Over the next few years, sacrifice, love, and devotion to each other and our cause served to unite us as a congregation. Unfortunately, this would not last. Soon, certain decisions would be made that would fracture our congregation and would forever change the lives of my wife and me.

My parents had also been struggling with the direction the leadership of the RLDS Church was taking the denomination. They and my two brothers (with their families) were a part of our group. Rather unexpectedly, my mother and father approached me one day and announced that they were going to Utah. (It is important to understand the feelings many of the RLDS membership had toward the LDS Church. The "Brighamites" were looked upon with quite a bit of condescension and suspicion by the RLDS. For many, Utah was a symbol, the stronghold and headquarters of the apostate denomination of

THE "BRIGHAMITES" WERE LOOKED UPON WITH QUITE A BIT OF CONDESCENSION AND SUSPICION BY THE RLDS.

the Restoration.) Why in the world would my parents be going to Utah, of all places? When I inquired, they simply responded, "We have to know if it is true." Puzzled by their remark, I asked, "Know if *what* is true?" "The Church," they responded. I was shocked to think they would even consider the Mormons as the "true Church." What in the world were they thinking?! They asked if I would go with them to investigate. I told them in no uncertain terms that I would not—that I could not. I had a deep love for and devotion to our group, and I knew the Mormonism couldn't be the "true Church." Contrary to my counsel, my parents rented a twelve-passenger van, and my two brothers and their families, with my mom and dad in tow, headed for Utah. The whole thing was quite puzzling to me. But confident in what we were doing in our group, I simply went back to my responsibilities there. One week later they returned and announced to my wife and I that The Church of Jesus Christ of Latter-day Saints was the "true Church." In only a few short days in Utah, they had met with missionaries and walked Temple Square. They had even gone to the LDS Church Office Building and asked to speak with "Brother Hinckley" (who was then serving as a counselor in the LDS First Presidency). Though President Hinckley was not available, another General Authority spent an afternoon with them, talking with them about the Church, and answering their questions. They had received a witness, decided to be baptized, and encouraged my wife and me to join them. When I indicated that I didn't believe that the Mormons were right, they urged me to get baptized anyway, and I could work on gaining a testimony of the LDS Church later. I informed them that I could never do that. I simply would not join a Church that I did not know to be true.

No doubt disappointed in my decision, my mother, father, and several other family members, began meeting with an LDS ward mission leader. They took the missionary discussions and set a baptismal date. Of course, I attended their baptismal service. It was surreal. How could they do this? My entire life I had been taught that the RLDS Church was true and that the LDS Church was teaching false doctrine. And now eleven members of my family were baptized and confirmed members of the LDS Church.

I didn't agree with their decision, but I certainly understood their desire to find something that could replace the loss of the faith of their fathers. They saw Mormonism as meeting that need; I saw my remnant group as meeting mine.

Satisfied that my parents and other family members had made the decision they thought best for them, I turned my attention back to the remnant congregation that I was so involved with. My wife and I were content there and imagined ourselves remaining active in the group—serving alongside of those whom we loved and worshipped with. With regularity, my five brethren in the priesthood and I would meet on Saturday mornings to plan worship services, activities, and other events. On one particular Saturday, I felt something was different. Things weren't as cordial as they traditionally had been. As I sat down at the table where we typically did our weekly planning, one of the men pointed at me and said, "We think you're teaching Mormon doctrine."

"WE THINK YOU'RE TEACHING MORMON DOCTRINE."

I was a bit taken aback, to say the least. I had been teaching a Book of Mormon class every Sunday to our group members, but in my estimation nothing had changed. It quickly became evident that my Book of Mormon class was not their primary worry. Rather, the other leaders of our group were concerned about the fact that so many of my family had joined the LDS Church. This had caused some to assume that I would shortly follow suit. I made it clear to them that I wasn't teaching anything contrary to what the group had espoused from the beginning, but it was clear that they had already made up their minds.

In the midst of all of this chaos and suspicion, I was supposed to give a talk to our group—a talk that had been scheduled prior to the leveling of these accusations. I asked my brothers if I was still going to be allowed to give the talk I was scheduled to deliver. They indicated that they would still allow me to do so, but they warned me, "Be careful what you say." I left the meeting that day in absolute disbelief. These were men I had worked with, served with, prayed with, and sacrificed with—and now we were being separated by misunderstanding, distrust, personal bias, and bigotry. What was happening to us? I could sense that everything we had worked toward and accomplished over the last few years was about to collapse.

I went home and told my wife about the meeting, the accusations, and my fears for the future. We wept as we contemplated the potential loss. Knowing there wasn't much that we could do, I turned my attention to preparing the talk that I was to give—the talk that would inevitably be the last one I would deliver to the group.

As I was preparing my remarks, the book of 1 Kings came to mind. In chapter 17, Elijah was instructed by the Lord to go to the brook Cherith, "And it shall be, that thou shalt drink of the brook; and I have commanded the ravens to feed thee there" (verse 4). As I thought about that verse, I felt that the Spirit was directing me, and I suddenly knew exactly what I was to say and do.

When the day I was to speak arrived, I stood before the congregation and informed them that I needed to leave the group for a while. I referenced the story in 1 Kings and then told them I needed to "go to the brook." I expressed my love for them and told them that they would remain in my prayers—as they had been from the beginning of our journey together. As I sat down, my best friend moved to the podium and announced, "Dennis Cato is under the influence of Satan." Not only had I not expected this, but I was at a loss as to how my message could have elicited such a response. I quietly picked up my books, walked off the rostrum, and gathered my wife and children. We walked out of the church, never to return.

As we returned home, I felt absolutely lost, bewildered, and spiritually crushed. What were we to do now? Where were we to turn? I felt directionless. I suppose one of the few things that enabled us to make it through this incredible trial in our lives was our testimony of the Book of Mormon and our firm belief in Joseph Smith as a prophet of God—two things the RLDS had largely moved away from.

At this point, there seemed to be few options for us as it related to a restoration community that we could worship with and feel a part of. During this period, I found meaning and purpose in a passage found in the ninth chapter of the book of Jeremiah, "Therefore thus saith the Lord of hosts, Behold, I will melt them, and try them" (verse 7) Similarly, Malachi 3:2 took on new meaning, "For he is like a refiner's fire." It seemed evident that my family was being spiritually refined, and prepared by the Lord for the direction He intended to take our lives. My wife and I continued to pray fervently, but we soon realized that the tenor of our prayers needed to change. Throughout our break from the RLDS Church—and during the establishment of our remnant group—our prayers largely consisted of requests that God would grant us success, growth, and continued blessings for the group. In a sense, I suppose, we were looking to justify our existence. But suddenly I felt that I had spiritually created a mess for my family; I had taken my wife and sons out of the RLDS Church, and now we

I FELT THAT I HAD SPIR-ITUALLY CREATED A MESS FOR MY FAMILY.

had left the group we had been a part of for four years. We found ourselves without a church and with nowhere to go. Because of our strong belief in Joseph Smith and the Book of Mormon, there simply weren't a plethora of Churches for us to turn to. What were we to do? I knew I couldn't afford to make another mistake. I approached Heavenly Father feeling lost and alone. Ultimately, this served a higher purpose, however, for my prayers dramatically changed through this trial. I was no longer concerned with what I wanted, but now I began to ask Heavenly Father what He wanted. For the first time in this process, I began to have a sense of what the Lord required of me. I had brought to my mind a passage from the Book of Mormon: "And I will tell you of the wrestle which I had before God, before I received a remission of my sins. . . . And my soul hungered; and I kneeled down before my Maker, and I cried unto him in mighty prayer and supplication" (Enos 1:2, 4). I now knew that the Lord was requiring of me a level of humility akin to that which was manifested by Enos. The prayers of our family could no longer be repetitive and general in nature, but, instead, they would need to be deeper, more heartfelt, and more faith-filled. If we were going to reap the blessings and direction we so desperately sought, we were going to have to become the type of disciples God needed. In the words of Elder Franklin D. Richards, of the Twelve, "Let us not forget . . . that they that would inherit the blessings of Abraham must do the works of Abraham, to entitle them to these blessings."[1] It seemed evident that our spiritual lives hung in the balance.

With what I knew of the Restoration and the joy I had found in the Book of Mormon (as a second witness of Jesus Christ), it became evident that my options were limited. I could not simply turn to *just any* Church. The next day I called the mission president of The Church of Jesus Christ of Latter-day Saints. I asked if he would send the missionaries to teach our family. Of course, we had many questions that needed to be answered. On the appointed evening of our first discussion, there was a knock at the door. When I opened the door, there stood two young men in white shirts and ties. They announced themselves as missionaries for the Church. That first night I probably overwhelmed them with my questions, and they took many notes. After discussing their doctrines for some time, they asked if they could come back in a few days. We indicated they could. When they returned a few days later, they brought their mission president with them.

For the next four weeks we regularly met with the missionaries and their mission president, and we made our way through each of the seven missionary discussions. As things progressed, I began to get a bit nervous because I knew that they would eventually ask us to set a date for baptism. I was dreading that moment, because I simply did not know that their Church was true. On one particular evening, as we neared the end of our discussion, the mission president asked me, "Do you want to know if it's true?" My answer came quickly, "Yes, I want to know." He stopped and looked me in the eye for quite some time, and I felt as though he was looking right through me. Again, he asked, "Do you *really* want to know

"DO YOU **REALLY** WANT TO KNOW **IT'S TRUE?**"

it's true?" My answer was, "I *have* to know if it's true." He then asked us to kneel and pray. One of the dear missionaries offered the prayer. I don't remember what was said, but as soon as the "amen" was pronounced, I started to get up off my knees. The mission president stopped me and asked, "How do you feel?" and I said that I felt fine. By the expression on his face, I could tell that was not the answer he was looking for. He then said, "Let's pray again." At the conclusion of the second prayer, we all stood. We did the cordial thing, hugging and shaking hands. But still I did not feel that I had received an answer regarding the LDS Church.

He then asked me a critical question, "Would you let these young elders give you a blessing?" This was a significant test for me, the crossroads of my conversion, really. I had been an elder in the RLDS Church and also in the remnant group. I firmly felt that I held the Melchizedek Priesthood. If I let these young men give me a blessing, I would be acknowledging *their* authority. To let them lay their hands upon me and pronounce a blessing would be a tacit acknowledgment that the Mormons have valid priesthood authority. How could I do this?

At the time, I didn't realize how very much God's hand was in this invitation to submit myself to the priesthood of these young missionaries.

GOD WAS CREATING THE PERFECT STORM.

However, as I look back, it is evident that God was creating the perfect storm. He was setting up the circumstance whereby my family and I would be converted to The Church of Jesus Christ of Latter-day Saints. At this point in our lives, we were so weary of fighting the turmoil that had followed us for years as we lost faith in our Church, thought we had found an alternative, and then had the rug pulled out from underneath us a second time. Yes, as I considered the mission president's invitation, I had to acknowledge within myself that I had felt the Spirit over the last four weeks. Whereas the RLDS Church's changes had brought turmoil and confusion, our time with the missionaries had brought into our lives peace and comfort. And so I found myself agreeing to receive a priesthood blessing from the elders. A chair was set in the middle of our family room, and the young elders stepped forward and placed their hands on my head. The first thing I noticed was that their hands were trembling. They were so scared. It was as though they too realized that this was the crossroad—this was the event that all of this had been pointing to. Miraculously, with the first words spoken in the blessing, I felt as though I was on top of a mountain and had taken a deep breath of pure, clean, fresh air. I had *never* felt such peace in my life. All the anger, confusion, and chaos from years of struggle were suddenly swept away. I was spiritually freed from the confusion that had

I HAD NEVER FELT SUCH PEACE IN MY LIFE.

been with me for many years. Through the priesthood, God's will for our family was clear. As soon as the final words of the blessing were uttered, I stood and announced that I wanted to be baptized.

Of course, the mission president wanted us to set a baptismal date right then and there. But I indicated that I could not. At that time, I was employed by a man in the remnant group we had been attending. I told the mission president that I would need to find a job before I could join the LDS Church, as I was sure that I would lose my only means of income once I got baptized. The mission president asked me if I had faith. I told him, "Of course I do, but I also have a family to support." I asked them to give me a little time to find a new job, and then we would be baptized. Again, he questioned my faith. My wife and I discussed what we should do, and determined that we would exercise our faith and move forward with our baptisms. Thus, on March 4, 1988, my wife and I, along with two of our sons (who were of age) were baptized into the LDS Church. Just as I had predicted, my employment was terminated only two days later. Yet, as evidence of God's grace and love, work was provided. That summer the Church historic sites needed workers. So for several months, during the daylight hours I planted flowers, mowed and trimmed lawns, and so on at various Church properties. In the evenings I worked as a security guard at a UPS facility. During this time, I didn't feel as blessed as I see, in retrospect, I truly was. Many nights I wondered why I had to lose my job—particularly when I acted in faith. I had done what God had asked me to do, even when it was against reason. Why was I not being blessed? But I was being blessed.

I HAD DONE WHAT GOD HAD ASKED ME TO DO, EVEN WHEN IT WAS AGAINST REASON.

Not only was God providing for us, but He was also setting up better employment for me. Only six months after losing my job, I found new employment, a job that paid 25 percent more than my previous job had. Again, it was evident that miracles were happening in our lives. I came to understand that, in all the world, He knows each one of us individually. He is always there for us and, even in the midst of the trials and tribulations of life, we are never alone.

Heavenly Father saved our spiritual lives. My family and I know where we came from, why we are here, and—through our faithfulness and obedience—where we will return. I promised Heavenly Father that if He would show me the way, I would work as hard as possible for as long as I'm allowed. Please know, this gospel is true. It brings healing, knowledge, and a joy beyond measure. I am grateful that families—*my family*—can be together forever. Our Lord and Savior, Jesus Christ, atoned for our sins. We will never be able to repay Him fully, but all He asks is that we give Him all we have and "He will make up the difference." This is my testimony, that He lives and through our leaders and scriptures we may truly know Him.

DENNIS

A LESSON TO BE LEARNED

Because religion is so central to who we are as human beings, the loss of one's faith can be absolutely devastating. One feels as though the rug has been pulled out from underneath him or her, and all that for so long seemed reliable and trustworthy suddenly comes into question. When one loses faith in one's religion, one often begins to doubt *everything*: not just the Church, but Christianity, the existence of God, long-held ethical beliefs, even relationships. Few life events are more life-changing than the loss of one's personal faith.

And yet, as President Cato's story suggests, sometimes the only thing that can change our spiritual trajectory in life *is* a crisis of faith. If we are committed to a belief system that is less than what God wants for us, sometimes the only way for Him to wake us up to something new—something bigger than we currently have—is to bring a little instability into our lives. If He can get our attention, He can recalibrate our direction.

For some, this is the way God gets us into the Church. For some, that divinely sent dissonance—and the fear of loss—is how He improves our marriage, or our relationship with a child. Sometimes this is the only way He can get us to change jobs. God is a master at using a crisis to get us pointed in the right direction. Thus the devastation is really a blessing in disguise.

ALONZO

NOTES

1. Franklin D. Richards, in *Journal of Discourses*, 24:337.

ROMAN CATHOLIC

BEVERLY MARBEN

I turned seventy this year and, as I look forward to enjoying another decade of life, I feel blessed to be able to do so with the direction, answers, and peace that I have enjoyed since my conversion to The Church of Jesus Christ of Latter-day Saints over forty-five years ago.

Before my conversion, I was an active Roman Catholic who, when I turned fifteen, left my parents and siblings to enter a convent, destined to live life as a nun—or so I **DESTINED TO LIVE LIFE AS A NUN.** thought. But, as is so often the case, God has His own plans for our lives, and this is the story of His plan for mine.

I have always been a logical person—one who seeks order in how I live. I love order! To me, everything is based on order. Cleaning puts dirt where it belongs; eating puts food where it belongs; reading puts words where they belong; and logical thinking puts all thoughts and reason in their place and order. Though logic and order are foundational to who I am, so is faith.

Indeed, I lived a very faith-filled childhood. When there were things I didn't understand, I trusted my loving mother and my Creator. When all else failed, I knew God knew all, and I knew that He knew me. He not only knew that I existed, but He knew that I wanted to please Him.

As a child, I had eleven older siblings and two younger siblings. My remarkable mother had fourteen children: eight girls and six boys. I was number twelve—"cheaper by the dozen," as they say. Though we were very poor, we really didn't know it since we lived in a poor neighborhood. Besides, our stay-at-home mother was very resourceful and hard working and, believe it or not, she spoiled us. She loved everything about being a mother, a wife, and a homemaker, and she had a "nonstop" relationship with Heavenly Father through her Catholic faith.

As children, my mother taught us integrity and virtue through living her life as a virtuous woman of integrity. In so many ways, it was my mother's example that contributed to me having a strong faith in God. She had a personal relationship with Heavenly Father that was visible in all she did and expressed in everything she said. My father also taught me many things by example, but they were mostly what *not* to do or say. He was always in ill health, made worse by his constant smoking and drinking. He would frequently put us down and, when he did so, my mother would always say to me, "Don't worry about what others say. You know who you are and God loves you. Just let others think they are right. But you know better."

My family didn't miss a Sunday attending Mass. Though my father never came, he would wait at home and listen to my mother's repeat of each weekly sermon. I loved hearing my mother's interpretation of what was said over the pulpit. She said it in words I understood.

Mom was a singer. At every Mass, it was the congregation's voices versus my mother's voice, and Mom always won out. My mother had a beautiful singing voice, but her dedication to the words made her singing even more pronounced. I politely asked her once, "Why don't you sing softer so you blend in with the congregation?" I will never forget her surprised response: "Why do I need to lower my standards? They need to raise theirs!" This was my mother. She loved the Lord and was not ashamed to show it.

> "WHY DO I NEED TO **LOWER MY STANDARDS?** THEY NEED TO **RAISE THEIRS!**"

Our family never owned a car. My father would walk to work every day. It seemed a long way from home, but he did it. Our groceries were purchased at a few stores in our neighborhood, and the Sears and Roebuck catalog took care of the rest. I remember one time waiting for a new pair of Sunday shoes, but, when they arrived they were too tight. There was no way I was going to go through the long wait for another delivery, so I suffered every Sunday without any expression of pain. My mother never knew about the plethora of bandages I used to comfort my aching feet. I never wanted to make my mother feel bad. I would rather suffer than let her know the shoes she got me weren't perfect. It was my little white lie that caused me to seriously deplete her first aid supplies.

Times were tough, and each of us gave a significant portion of any earnings we had to our parents. With such a large family, it was considered everyone's responsibility to contribute. Even a portion of my babysitting money went to supporting the family.

As a family, we managed just fine without a car; we each got around walking or by bus. The Catholic Church and school were on the same grounds, just a few blocks from home. Each school day started with a Mass, so technically (during the school year) I attended church six days a week. I *always* had trouble getting to Mass on time. I had a hard time getting up when my mother would wake me each morning. I suppose this was due to the fact that, having so many siblings and a small house, I never had my own room. In fact, I never had my own bed. Three of us slept in a double bed, so staying in bed later than everyone else was my only time to be alone.

STAYING IN BED LATER THAN EVERYONE ELSE WAS MY ONLY TIME TO BE ALONE.

My being so consistently late for Mass was a constant concern to the nuns and also an ironic situation since I cannot remember a time I didn't want to be one of *them*. You would think that, for a girl who wanted to be a nun, punctuality in arriving to church would be natural—but not for me. I always loved opportunities to act on my faith. But as obedient as I was, I still had a bit of a rebel in me. I didn't like it when the nuns pointed out that I was late for Mass, particularly since I was never late for *school*. Sure, if there wasn't Mass, I would have been late for school (since school followed Mass), but I wanted credit for never being late to class. In my mind, church was church and school was school. Unfortunately, the nuns didn't see it that way.

When I was five years old, my mother took me on a seven-hour trip by train to Wilmette, Illinois. I was the only one of the kids that got to go with her because I could ride for free if I sat on her lap the entire time. She made the trip to visit my sixteen-year-old sister, who was living in a convent, preparing to be a nun. (It was the same convent I would enter ten years later.) The order was called the "Sisters of Christian Charity, Daughters of the Blessed Virgin Mary of the Immaculate Conception."

My sister wasn't happy in the convent, largely because she had come to the realization that she might not qualify as a teacher (in a teaching order) and, thus, her only other option would be to spend the rest of her life in the "mother house"—which was the main property. If that became her lot, then she would spend her years doing domestic chores to ensure the property was kept clean and in good order. She didn't become a nun so that she could live her life as a maid—but that looked like what she might have to do. After two years in the convent, the nuns felt that she was struggling emotionally, and so they sent her home. Upon her return to my parents' house, I remember her telling me stories about how strict the rules of the convent were. These stories just made me want to be a nun all the more.

My entire childhood I wanted to show Heavenly Father how much I loved Him, how much I cared about others, and how much I did not want to get caught up in the ways of the world. I wanted to be the best I could be and, as a Catholic (living in the 1960s), it didn't get better than aspiring to be a nun.

I kept this secret locked within my heart and head. I never told anyone about my desire until I absolutely had to. It was too personal, too sacred. I didn't want anyone to tamper with my heart and soul. But I longed to be there—to be in the convent—to be a nun. I remember a time in fourth grade that I could barely stand the thought that I had to wait until I graduated from the eighth grade before I could enter. I would talk non-stop to God about my plan, and I remember telling Him, "I am pretty young and may be foolish, so if I am making a mistake, get me out! I will never leave the convent on my own. I will never give up this dream—*never!* So, if you have other plans, you need to let me know that."

I LONGED TO BE THERE— TO BE IN THE **CONVENT**— TO BE A **NUN.**

When I was finally an eighth grader, I knew I had to tell my parents about my desire to become a nun. I don't remember much about that day other than waiting in the "girls'" room until it appeared that everyone was well settled. As I made what felt like an endless trip downstairs to tell my parents, I thought the pounding of my heart would startle them before I even entered the room. I felt like I might not live through the experience. I had practiced every word; every sentence was well planned, and I feared that any glitch in the presentation might send me over the edge. As always, my mother was wonderful and wise. Her only question was simply, "Are you sure?" I have no memory of my father's response. It must have been one of acceptance, since it would have been a traumatic night if he had much to say. (To his credit, I know deep in his heart my father loved his children—though, growing up, it was too deep for us to see.)

I wasn't the only girl graduating from the eighth grade that would be entering the convent; there were three of us. This made the long trip bearable, and the tearful separation from family more manageable. During my time in the convent, I made a total of eight trips to the convent and eight trips home. Each time I left my family was a tearful experience, and most visits home were joyful. Every trip home my friends and I were so happy, we couldn't help ourselves—as our numbers increased, we would sing the most beautiful harmonies to the folks traveling on the train. They always seemed quite pleased by this. We couldn't have been happier, and our happiness was contagious.

My first year in the convent, we stayed the entire school year, including the Christmas break. However, my next year, we were allowed to go home for two weeks (during the Christmas holiday). The first-year girls were thrilled at the news that they would be allowed to go home for the holiday. Those of us who had experienced a Christmas in the convent, however, weren't necessarily as excited about the change in policy. If you haven't experienced it, there isn't really anything to compare it to, but Christmas in the convent was one of the most spiritually uplifting experiences you can imagine. For me, it was the most profoundly spiritual experience I had enjoyed to that point in my young life. Everything about the holiday was spiritual, as every effort was made to focus on the true meaning of Christ's birth. It was heavenly! And nothing about going home, not even seeing family, could make up for not being there and reliving that experience during my second Christmas in the convent.

It was hard to be home after living in the ceremony and size of the convent. My parents' house was decidedly disciplined, though unceremonious and small. At home, I thought the walls were closing in and the ceiling was coming down on me. Even the convent bathrooms (which were the smallest rooms there) were bigger than *any* room in my parents' home. Then there was the lack of order. In the convent, everything had its time and place. It was a house of order—and I love order! But at home, we ate whenever, we talked out of turn, there were no bells to signal change, we had to make decisions on clothing, there was no designated time to sleep and rise, and so on. I was so adjusted to convent living that all the world's choices were exhausting and felt totally unnecessary in the God-centered life I had freely chosen. The summers gave me time to adjust to being

ALL THE **WORLD'S CHOICES** WERE **EXHAUSTING** AND FELT TOTALLY **UNNECESSARY** IN THE **GOD-CENTERED LIFE.**

home, but they also made it hard to go back. Two weeks at Christmas was not enough time to get out of the habit of living a life of order. For me, to "not be of the world" (see John 17:16; Romans 12:2), was something I took quite literally! I had no problem leaving "the world." A life with God was glorious!

I was happy in the convent. I followed the rules faithfully, and even found ways to go above and beyond what was expected. If something was considered "challenging," I did it faithfully, and then just a little bit more.

There were times and places where total silence was required. For example, we were never to speak in the hallways, as the chapel doors were always open. Consequently, the hallways were considered an extension of the chapel. I had no trouble with the silence, though some might be surprised by that, as I *do* thrive on conversation. In the morning and evening we said our prayers aloud. We had daily Mass (and *yes*, I was on time—though I was usually at the end of the line). I was told to arise when the bell rang, and I did. I was told to make a perfect bed, and I did. I was told to have my small curtained off area in order, and I did. I never compromised what was expected of me. I just learned how to obey the rules with more speed.

During the four years I was there, I completed my high school education. Those of us who were still high school students were called "Aspirants" (aspiring to be nuns). Then, in the summer of 1965, I received my "candidate" title (which meant I was an official candidate for membership in our "order"). There was a ceremony at church, and each candidate was presented a modified nun's habit. The official habit of this order covered every part of the body except the hands, neck and face. Even the forehead and below the chin were covered. We were allowed to show some hair, as the veil was attached to a headband that exposed the very front of our hair. At this time, I gave away every earthly possession that I had, and I accepted that any gifts I received would be community property, belonging to the order—not to me. I was very happy to be in this next step in a life of dedication to the Lord.

Being a candidate was much stricter, but it was what I wanted. We could only talk for an hour in the morning and an hour at night. Bells would signal when we could begin and when we were to end our communicating. We were assigned to work in the gardens and to harvest the crops. We were busy with chores, even while we continued our training. We were required to take a number of tests for the purpose of allowing the nuns in charge to know us better, and so that we could progress toward taking our final vows. The tests took three days to complete and, as part of the process, we each met with a psychologist. (His physical appearance struck me as rather entertaining, as the convent was seriously monochromatic, and he was seriously not.) He looked threatened by the stark nothingness of our environment, and he seemed to want everyone to know he was not one of us. (As though any of us were confused about that!)

The tests came and went and, on October 3, 1965, we individually met with our Mistress—the nun in charge. She looked extremely serious as she granted permission for me to enter her office. She started out by saying, "God works in mysterious ways." I agreed! She then said, "The psychologist doesn't think this is your vocation." I laughed. That was clearly not the right response, as she looked startled, and appeared as though she couldn't continue the conversation. I was beyond puzzled. I wondered,

"THE **PSYCHOLOGIST DOESN'T THINK** THIS IS YOUR VOCATION."

Why does it matter what he *thinks?* My calling came from God, not a psychologist. Through her strained expressions, she said, "We will notify your parents." Well, that said it all! NOTIFY MY PARENTS? Parents were *never* notified! I nearly died from pneumonia and they didn't bother to call my parents! But a psychologist dressed like a clown isn't sure if I should be a nun, and so they're going to call my parents?

I don't remember anything else she said, though I could see that she was still talking. I had to process what I had just been told and try to embrace the fact that they were going to let me go. I would be a reject and, as it happened, excluded from the other girls that had both passed the written tests and received the blessing of the psychologist. The psychological assessment and tests had never been done before. I found out years later that they almost ruled out the results when they saw that I was on the "send-her-home" list. When I got over the shock, I remembered the agreement I had made with God: "Find a way to get me out, if I am making a mistake. I will never leave on my own." So, since I knew God—*not the psychologist*—was in charge, I felt comforted, though all of this was still very hard to take.

SINCE **I KNEW GOD—NOT** THE **PSYCHOLOGIST—** WAS **IN CHARGE, I** FELT **COMFORTED.**

We were not allowed to tell anyone that we were being sent home. The next day I was told that, after dinner, I should pack my trunk. I would be leaving on Tuesday. Everyone else was told I wasn't feeling well and that I had gone to bed early. I did as I was told. The next morning, I finished my last assignment in the kitchen and then sat in the front parlor while I waited for someone to drive me to the Evanston, Illinois, train station. I found out later that the reason they waited until the very last minute to get me to the train station was because they were trying to contact my parents. As it happened, my parents were called five hours before my seven-hour train trip ended. The convent sent me off without knowing if someone would be there at the station to receive me.

I didn't have a dime to make a call. I didn't even know where my family lived because they had moved after I left, and I wasn't planning on going back home for another six years. The nuns had prepared food for me to take on the train, but they forgot to give it to me, so I had nothing to eat during my lengthy trip. I arrived home, still wearing my habit—as it was the only clothing I had. This was my last trip home, and it was a sad one for me. I was assured in my heart that this was an answer to that prayer I had offered as a little girl, but it came too suddenly and the nuns handled it without sensitivity. I was nineteen.

I don't remember how the first few days went, as I adjusted to "non-convent" life. I do remember trying to acquire a few basic things, like clothes. One of my brothers immediately found me a job working at his business, and I plugged myself back into the world. I worked long hours over the next few non-eventful years. My whole world consisted of work and home-life. My younger sister, Lynda, made the adjustment manageable, for which I am grateful.

It was hard for me to be just a parishioner. It was not enough—not fulfilling—but it was all I had. There were times I wanted to sit in church and talk to God but, because of vandalism, they started locking the doors during the day. I felt shut out in body and soul. Everything about my life had been God-centered. Suddenly, I had to find ways to fit Him in. It was unbearably hard.

I met my future husband March 1, 1968. It was as if we had known each other before and, as we talked, it was like we were catching up on lost time—like we were old friends. We were both surprised by this. It didn't make sense. But I ended up falling in love with him, even though he was a controlling man that lacked sensitivity. There was a part of my "convent" brain that still remained with me, the part that wanted to have someone control me and allow me to be obedient. He fit the bill perfectly! I also knew that he needed me and that I could give him the patience and consideration he needed from a strong woman like me. I saw myself as the one who could develop his potential

HE WAS SUPPOSED TO BE **PART OF MY** **TIME** ON **EARTH.**

(though I shouldn't have "stuck it out" for thirty-seven years). As hard as the marriage was, I really did feel he was supposed to be part of my time on earth. I truly feel we knew each other in the pre-earth life.

We married quickly—the same year we met, and our daughter was born the following year. My husband was a very sad person, and I made every effort to bring happiness to his heart and soul. Unfortunately, he was emotionally and physically abusive. It was an unending slow process that eventually took over my brain, and I found myself trapped in his misery. I lived in a nightmare world, but I never allowed my circumstances to take away my connection to God and my desire to be worthy of Heavenly Father's love. Then, when I thought things couldn't get worse, they did.

I FOUND MYSELF TRAPPED IN HIS MISERY.

In 1971, my husband was working for the airlines and we had just bought a new car when the airlines went on strike. Jobs were hard to come by and so he ended up getting a job as a security guard at a UPS store. I took a job working at a bank, reconciling accounts at night. Both our jobs didn't come close to what we had been making prior to the strike, and his depression got worse. Though this seemed like such a sad time, it was actually a miracle and blessing in disguise.

While he worked at UPS, there was a repeat customer that he started to build up a relationship with. The man had his own business selling Shaklee products, and he convinced my husband to do the same. So one evening he came over to our home to tell us about the business. We heard all about the products and how they would better our lives. He told us about how we could earn decent money as distributors running our own business. Since money was a concern for us at the time, it all sounded good. We talked and talked, and then everything took a turn.

This Shaklee-selling person was also a Mormon and, without noticing the transition from selling things to believing things, we had our first discussion about The Church of Jesus Christ of Latter-day Saints.

I HAD NEVER SEEN HIM EMBRACE GOODNESS SO COMFORTABLY—SO EXCITEDLY.

What surprised me the most was my husband's reaction to such a personal and Godly conversation. I had never seen him embrace goodness so comfortably—so excitedly. He wanted to hear more, so the missionaries were scheduled to take over on another night. I don't think I was anywhere near as excited as he was, as I already had a relationship with God. It appeared he had just found his, as he never practiced any faith before this.

I never imagined that this was going to change *my* life. But in the process, the Holy Ghost spoke to my "longing-for-answers" soul. For example, I had always wondered but never understood why we all start living life in very different situations, even though we are all working toward the same goal—to get back to Heavenly Father. If life was essentially like a board game, we would all start in the same place on the board, and we would all have the same rules and potential rewards. But life wasn't like that, and I often wondered why. Then the missionaries told us that we lived before we came to earth and that we came here at a time and place in accordance with our progress in the pre-earth life. They testified that this life is not the beginning of our existence. "Yes! Of course I lived with Heavenly Father before I was known as child number twelve!" I thought to myself. Of course I knew my husband before I met him here on earth! (That could explain our instant connection.) I realized that I brought my closeness to Heavenly Father with me from the pre-mortal life. My logical brain was bursting at the seams, and my happy heart pounded out of my chest as the missionaries taught us. At that very moment, questions I had never been able to answer were suddenly answered. Things I thought I would always just have to "trust in faith" now were knowledge. I was converted!

THINGS I THOUGHT I WOULD ALWAYS JUST HAVE TO "TRUST IN FAITH" NOW WERE KNOWLEDGE.

My husband wanted to get baptized even before the discussions were completed. Much to my surprise, when I told people at work that I was going to get baptized into the Mormon Church, they were horrified! Their intense feelings shocked me, particularly since we were just coworkers. When I told my husband about their reaction, he said, "Maybe that's a sign we are making a mistake!" The minute he said that I realized that my coworkers' visceral reaction was the adversary trying to stop us from having the gospel of Jesus Christ in our lives. When I expressed this sentiment to my husband, he agreed.

We were baptized April 3, 1971—exactly five and a half years after I was told the psychologist didn't think being a nun was my vocation. We were baptized by that Shaklee salesman, whose testimony touched my troubled husband. I see now that if he hadn't embraced the gospel—as controlling as he was—he would not have let me embrace it. If his heart had not been touched first—I do not believe I would have been allowed to embrace what I now knew to be true. He didn't remain active in the Church for long. The commitment required was just too much for him.

However, he allowed me to continue to be active and to rear our two daughters in the Church. He was never able to settle his heart. Yet, I feel blessed that he *did* open it to the gospel long enough that it was thereby made available to me.

I have learned so much about myself and my relationship with Heavenly Father and His Son Jesus Christ through the various callings I have had over the last forty-five years—including my first calling as a primary teacher. My husband and I divorced in 2005, and I was able to serve a twenty-three-month senior mission in California. I've taught seminary, been a Relief Society President, and now—once again—I am a Primary teacher. In 1988 I received my temple endowment, which has been a tremendous blessing in my life and a covenant I am grateful that my husband allowed me to make.

It struck me not too long ago that I had spent six years in full-time service to the Lord: four in a convent and two as an LDS missionary. Having just completed my sixth decade on this earth, I have tithed my life—giving 10 percent of it in full-time service.

I HAVE **TITHED MY LIFE**— GIVING **10 PERCENT** OF IT IN **FULL-TIME SERVICE.**

I have a very strong testimony of the gospel. For years I thought the only way to be close to Heavenly Father was to put everything else aside. I see now that those years in the convent were exactly where I was supposed to be at the time. There was a challenging life ahead for me, and my convent years helped me to cleanse from childhood negativity and ingrain God's love so deep in my heart that I would survive my journey leading me to The Church of Jesus Christ of Latter-day Saints. I once tried to be a *nun*, but I am now a *sister*. I am Sister Marben, and I am a Mormon.

I AM **SISTER MARBEN,** AND I AM **A MORMON.**

By way of testimony, I will conclude with the scripture I put on my missionary plaque: "And . . . he doth require that ye should do as he hath commanded you; for which if ye do, he doth immediately bless you; and therefore he hath paid you. And ye are still indebted unto him, and are, and will be, forever and ever; therefore, of what have ye to boast?" (Mosiah 2:24).

BEV

A LESSON TO BE LEARNED

Three times in the Doctrine and Covenants the Lord commands that we "seek learning, even by study and also by faith" (D&C 88:118; 109:7, 14). To Oliver Cowdery, the Lord promised, "I will tell you in your mind and in your heart, by the Holy Ghost" (D&C 8:2), implying that revelation not only *feels right* (heart), but often *makes sense* (mind). Indeed, for many who convert to the Church, there is a cerebral side to their conversion—as there was for Bev. While God will occasionally ask us to do something that seems counter-intuitive, more often than not, His counsels are logical. They make sense!

It is important that each of us develop the faith to act when God calls upon us to do so. And the man or woman who develops sufficient faith in God to act—even when they cannot see the reason behind the revelation—is to be commended. Such is a great gift! Yet, the words of the hymn, "Lead, Kindly Light," come to mind: "Keep thou my feet; I do not ask to see. The distant scene—one step enough for me."[1] In the hymn, we commit to move toward that which we do not see. However, the caveat is found in the line, "One step enough for me." In other words, we promise the Lord we will move forward largely in the dark—if He will but give us a small bit of information, just a smidgen of logic or reason that will make moving forward both feel right and also seem right.

When one surveys the entirety of the gospel landscape, there is much to be seen that logically confirms the rightness of our conversion. Such is always the case!

ALONZO

NOTES

1.   "Lead, Kindly Light," *Hymns*, no. 97.

ABOUT THE COMPILER

Alonzo L. Gaskill was an altar boy in the Greek Orthodox Church before becoming a member of The Church of Jesus Christ of Latter-day Saints, a best-selling author, and a professor of Church history and doctrine. Gaskill holds a bachelor's degree in philosophy, a master's in theology, and a PhD in biblical studies. Gaskill has taught at Brigham Young University (BYU) since 2003. Prior to coming to BYU, he served in a variety of assignments within the Church Educational System—most recently as the director of the LDS Institute of Religion at Stanford University (1995–2003).

ISBN 978-1-4621-2008-6   USA $18.99 CAN $21.99

51899

9 781462 120086

CFI
AN IMPRINT OF
CEDAR FORT, INC.

CEDAR FORT
Publishing & Media

WWW.CEDARFORT.COM   WWW.ALONZOGASKILL.WORDPRESS.COM